CLASSICS IN PSYCHOLOGY

CLASSICS IN PSYCHOLOGY

Advisory Editors
HOWARD GARDNER
AND
JUDITH KREIGER GARDNER

Editorial Board
Wayne Dennis
Paul A. Kolers
Sheldon H. White

A NOTE ABOUT THE AUTHOR

HUGO MÜNSTERBERG was born in Danzig in 1863, and educated at Geneva and Leipzig. He took his doctorate in psychology with Wundt and later took a degree in medicine at Heidelberg. William James was very impressed with Münsterberg's scholarship and induced him to come to Harvard in 1892 and to direct the psychological laboratory. Except for a short hiatus, Münsterberg remained at Harvard until his death during World War I in 1916.

Though Münsterberg began his career as a proponent of Wundt's psychology, he gradually drew away from theoretical and empirical studies of sensation, perception, and thought. Instead, he became interested in applications of psychology, in psychotherapy, legal psychology, political psychology, and industrial psychology. In the view of many, it was Münsterberg who founded the field of "applied" psychology.

PSYCHOLOGY AND
INDUSTRIAL EFFICIENCY

BY

HUGO MÜNSTERBERG

ARNO PRESS
A New York Times Company
New York ★ 1973

Reprint Edition 1973 by Arno Press Inc.

Reprinted from a copy in
The University of Illinois Library

Classics in Psychology
ISBN for complete set: 0-405-05130-1
See last pages of this volume for titles.

Manufactured in the United States of America

———◆———

Library of Congress Cataloging in Publication Data

Münsterberg, Hugo, 1863-1916.
    Psychology and industrial efficiency.

    (Classics in psychology)
    Reprint of the 1913 ed. published by Houghton
Mifflin, Boston.
    1. Psychology, Industrial. I. Title.
II. Series. [DNLM: BFM949p 1913F]
HF5548.8.M77 1973b   158.7   73-2979
ISBN 0-405-05151-4

PSYCHOLOGY AND
INDUSTRIAL EFFICIENCY

PSYCHOLOGY AND
INDUSTRIAL EFFICIENCY

BY

HUGO MÜNSTERBERG

BOSTON AND NEW YORK

HOUGHTON MIFFLIN COMPANY

The Riverside Press Cambridge

1913

TO

HAROLD F. McCORMICK

PREFATORY NOTE

THIS book corresponds to a German book, which I published a few months ago, under the title *Psychologie und Wirtschaftsleben: Ein Beitrag zur angewandten Experimental-Psychologie* (Leipzig: J. A. Barth). It is not a translation, as some parts of the German volume have been abbreviated or entirely omitted and other parts have been enlarged and supplemented. Yet the essential substance of the two books is identical.

CONTENTS

vii

CONTENTS

INTRODUCTION

PSYCHOLOGY AND INDUSTRIAL EFFICIENCY

INTRODUCTION

I

APPLIED PSYCHOLOGY

OUR aim is to sketch the outlines of a new science which is to intermediate between the modern laboratory psychology and the problems of economics: the psychological experiment is systematically to be placed at the service of commerce and industry. So far we have only scattered beginnings of the new doctrine, only tentative efforts and disconnected attempts which have started, sometimes in economic, and sometimes in psychological, quarters. The time when an exact psychology of business life will be presented as a closed and perfected system lies very far distant. But the earlier the attention of wider circles is directed to its beginnings and to the importance and bearings of its tasks, the quicker and the more sound will be the development of this young science. What is most needed to-day at the beginning of the new movement are

clear, concrete illustrations which demonstrate
the possibilities of the new method. In the following pages, accordingly, it will be my aim to analyze the results of experiments which have actually been carried out, experiments belonging to
many different spheres of economic life. But these
detached experiments ought always at least to
point to a connected whole; the single experiments
will, therefore, always need a general discussion
of the principles as a background. In the interest
of such a wider perspective we may at first enter
into some preparatory questions of theory. They
may serve as an introduction which is to lead
us to the actual economic life and the present
achievements of experimental psychology.

It is well known that the modern psychologists
only slowly and very reluctantly approached the
apparently natural task of rendering useful service to practical life. As long as the study of the
mind was entirely dependent upon philosophical
or theological speculation, no help could be expected from such endeavors to assist in the daily
walks of life. But half a century has passed since
the study of consciousness was switched into the
tracks of exact scientific investigation. Five
decades ago the psychologists began to devote
themselves to the most minute description of the
mental experiences and to explain the mental life

in a way which was modeled after the pattern of exact natural sciences. Their aim was no longer to speculate about the soul, but to find the psychical elements and the constant laws which control their connections. Psychology became experimental and physiological. For more than thirty years the psychologists have also had their workshops. Laboratories for experimental psychology have grown up in all civilized countries, and the new method has been applied to one group of mental traits after another. And yet we stand before the surprising fact that all the manifold results of the new science have remained book knowledge, detached from any practical interests. Only in the last ten years do we find systematic efforts to apply the experimental results of psychology to the needs of society.

It is clear that the reason for this late beginning is not an unwillingness of the last century to make theoretical knowledge serviceable to the demands of life. Every one knows, on the contrary, that the glorious advance of the natural sciences became at the same time a triumphal march of technique. Whatever was brought to light in the laboratories of the physicists and chemists, of the physiologists and pathologists, was quickly transformed into achievements of physical and chemical industry, of medicine and hygiene, of agriculture and mining and transportation. No realm of the external social life remained untouched. The scientists, on the other hand, felt that the far-reaching practical effect which came from their discoveries exerted a stimulating influence on the theoretical researches themselves. The pure search for truth and knowledge was not lowered when the electrical waves were harnessed for wireless telegraphy, or the Roentgen rays were forced into the service of surgery. The knowledge of nature and the mastery of nature have always belonged together.

The persistent hesitation of the psychologists to make similar practical use of their experimental results has therefore come from different causes. The students of mental life evidently had the feeling that quiet, undisturbed research was needed for the new science of psychology in order that a certain maturity might be reached before a contact with the turmoil of practical life would be advisable. The sciences themselves cannot escape injury if their results are forced into the rush of the day before the fundamental ideas have been cleared up, the methods of investigation really tried, and an ample supply of facts collected. But this very justified reluctance becomes a real danger if it grows into an instinctive fear of coming into contact at all with practical life. To be sure, in any single case there may be a difference of opinion as to when the right time has come and when the inner consolidation of a new science is sufficiently advanced for the technical service, but it ought to be clear that it is not wise to wait until the scientists have settled all the theoretical problems involved. True progress in every scientific field means that the problems become multiplied and that ever new questions keep coming to the surface. If the psychologists were to refrain from practical application until the theoretical results of their laboratories need no supplement, the time for applied psychology would never come. Whoever looks without prejudice on the development of modern psychology ought to acknowledge that the hesitancy which was justified in the beginning would to-day be inexcusable lack of initiative. For the sciences of the mind, too, the time has come when theory and practice must support each other. An exceedingly large mass of facts has been gathered, the methods have become refined and differentiated, and however much may still be under discussion, the ground common to all is ample enough to build upon.

Another important reason for the slowness of practical progress was probably this. When the psychologists began to work with the new experimental methods, their most immediate concern was to get rid of mere speculation and to take hold of actual facts. Hence they regarded the natural sciences as their model, and, together with the experimental method which distinguishes scientific work, the characteristic goal of the sciences was accepted too. This scientific goal is always the attainment of general laws; and so it happened that in the first decades after the foundation of psychological laboratories the general laws of the mind absorbed the entire attention and interest of the investigators. The result of such an attitude was, that we learned to understand the working of the typical mind, but that all the individual variations were almost neglected. When the various individuals differed in their mental behavior, these differences appeared almost as disturbances which the psychologists had to eliminate in order to find the general laws which hold for every mind. The studies were accordingly confined to the general averages of mental experience, while the variations from such averages were hardly included in the scientific account. In earlier centuries, to be sure, the interest of the psychological observers had been given almost entirely to the rich manifoldness of human characters and intelligences and talents. In the new period of experimental work, this interest was taken as an indication of the unscientific fancies of the earlier age, in which the curious and the anecdotal attracted the view. The new science which was to seek the laws was to overcome such popular curiosity. In this sign experimental psychology has conquered. The fundamental laws of the ideas and of the attention, of the memory and of the will, of the feeling and of the emotions, have been elaborated. Yet it slowly became evident that such one-sidedness, however necessary it may have been at the beginning, would make any practical application impossible. In practical life we never have to do with what is common to all human beings, even when we are to influence large masses; we have to deal with personalities whose mental life is characterized by particular traits of nationality, or race, or vocation, or sex, or age, or special interests, or other features by which they differ from the average mind which the theoretical psychologist may construct as a type. Still more frequently we have to act with reference to smaller groups or to single individuals whose mental physiognomy demands careful consideration. As long as experimental psychology remained essentially a science of the mental laws, common to all human beings, an adjustment to the practical demands of daily life could hardly come in question. With such general laws we could never have mastered the con-

INTRODUCTION

crete situations of society, because we should have had to leave out of view the fact that there are gifted and ungifted, intelligent and stupid, sensitive and obtuse, quick and slow, energetic and weak individuals.

But in recent years a complete change can be traced in our science. Experiments which refer to these individual differences themselves have been carried on by means of the psychological laboratory, at first reluctantly and in tentative forms, but within the last ten years the movement has made rapid progress. To-day we have a psychology of individual variations from the point of view of the psychological laboratory.[1] This development of schemes to compare the differences between the individuals by the methods of experimental science was after all the most important advance toward the practical application of psychology. The study of the individual differences itself is not applied psychology, but it is the presupposition without which applied psychology would have remained a phantom.

II

THE DEMANDS OF PRACTICAL LIFE

WHILE in this way the progress of psychology itself and the development of the psychology of individual differences favored the growth of applied psychology, there arose at the same time an increasing demand in the midst of practical life. Especially the teachers and the physicians, later the lawyers as well, looked for help from exact psychology. The science of education and instruction had always had some contact with the science of the mind, as the pedagogues could never forget that the mental development of the child has to stand in the centre of educational thought. For a long while pedagogy was still leaning on a philosophical psychology, after that old-fashioned study of the soul had been given up in psychological quarters. At last, in the days of progressive experimental psychology, the time came when the teachers under the pressure of their new needs began to inquire how far the modern laboratory could aid them in the classroom. The pedagogical psychology of memory, of attention, of will, and of intellect was systematically worked up by men with practical

school interests. We may notice in the movement a slow but most important shifting. At first
the results of theoretical psychology were simply
transplanted into the pedagogical field. Experiments which were carried on in the interest of
pure theoretical science were made practical use
of, but their application remained a mere chance
by-product. Only slowly did the pedagogical
problems themselves begin to determine the experimental investigation. The methods of laboratory psychology were applied for the solving of
those problems which originated in the school experience, and only when this point was reached
could a truly experimental pedagogy be built on a
psychological foundation. We stand in the midst
of this vigorous and healthy movement, which
has had a stimulating effect on theoretical psychology itself.

We find a similar situation in the sphere of the
physician. He could not pass by the new science
of the mind without instinctively feeling that his
medical diagnosis and therapy could be furthered
in many directions by the experimental method.
Not only the psychiatrist and nerve specialist,
but in a certain sense every physician had made
use of a certain amount of psychology in his professional work. He had always had to make clear
to himself the mental experiences of the patient,

to study his pain sensations and his feelings of comfort, his fears and his hopes, his perceptions and his volitions, and to a certain degree he had always tried to influence the mental life of the patient, to work on him by suggestion and to help him by stimulating his mind. But as far as a real description and explanation of such mental experiences came in question, all remained a dilettantic semi-psychology which worked with the most trivial conceptions of popular thinking. The medical men recognized the disproportion between the exactitude of their anatomical, physiological, and pathological observation and the superficiality of their self-made psychology. Thus the desire arose in their own medical circle to harmonize their psychological means of diagnosis and therapy with the schemes of modern scientific psychology. The physician who examines the sensations in a nervous disease, or the intelligence in a mental disease, or heals by suggestion or hypnotism, tries to apply the latest discoveries of the psychological laboratory. But here, too, the same development as in pedagogy can be traced. The physicians at first made use only of results which had been secured under entirely different points of view, but later the experiments were subordinated to the special medical problems. Then the physician was no longer obliged simply

13

to use what he happened to find among the results of the theoretical psychologist, but carried
on the experiments in the service of medical problems. The independent status of experimental
medical psychology could be secured only by this
development.

In somewhat narrower limits the same may
be said as to the problems of law. A kind of popular psychology was naturally involved whenever
judges or lawyers analyzed the experience on the
witness stand or discussed the motives of crime
or the confessions of the criminal or the social
conditions of criminality. But when every day
brought new discoveries in the psychological laboratory, it seemed natural to make use of the new
methods and of the new results in the interest of
the courtroom. The power of observation in the
witness, the exactitude of his memory, the character of his illusions and imagination, his suggestibility and his feeling, appeared in a new light in
view of the experimental investigations, and the
emotions and volitions of the criminal were understood with a new insight. Here, too, the last step
was taken. Instead of being satisfied with experiments which the psychologist had made for his
own purposes, the students of legal psychology
adjusted experiments to the particular needs of
the courtroom. Investigations were carried on to

determine the fidelity of testimony or to find methods for the detection of hidden thoughts and so on. Efforts toward the application of psychology have accordingly grown up in the fields of pedagogy, medicine, and jurisprudence, but as these studies naturally do not remain independent of one another, they all together form the one unified science of applied psychology.[2]

As soon as the independence of this new science was felt, it was natural that new demands and new problems should continue to originate within its own limits. There must be applied psychology wherever the investigation of mental life can be made serviceable to the tasks of civilization. Criminal law, education, medicine, certainly do not constitute the totality of civilized life. It is therefore the duty of the practical psychologist systematically to examine how far other purposes of modern society can be advanced by the new methods of experimental psychology. There is, for instance, already far-reaching agreement that the problems of artistic creation, of scientific observation, of social reform, and many similar endeavors must be acknowledged as organic parts of applied psychology. Only one group of purposes is so far surprisingly neglected in the realm of the psychological laboratory: the purposes of the economic life, the purposes of commerce and

INTRODUCTION

industry, of business and the market in the widest sense of the word. The question how far applied psychology can be extended in this direction is the topic of the following discussions.

III

APPLIED psychology is evidently to be classed with the technical sciences. It may be considered as psychotechnics, since we must recognize any science as technical if it teaches us to apply theoretical knowledge for the furtherance of human purposes. Like all technical sciences, applied psychology tells us what we ought to do if we want to reach certain ends; but we ought to realize at the threshold where the limits of such a technical science lie, as they are easily overlooked, with resulting confusion. We must understand that every technical science says only: you must make use of this means, if you wish to reach this or that particular end. But no technical science can decide within its limits whether the end itself is really a desirable one. The technical specialist knows how he ought to build a bridge or how he ought to pierce a tunnel, presupposing that the bridge or the tunnel is desired. But whether they are desirable or not is a question which does not concern the technical scientist, but which must be considered from economic or political or other points of view. Everywhere the engineer must know how to reach an end, and must leave it to others to settle whether the end is in itself desirable. Often the end may be a matter of course for every reasonable being. The extreme case is presented by the applied science of medicine, where the physician subordinates all his technique to the end of curing the patient. Yet if we are consistent we must acknowledge that all his medical knowledge can prescribe to him only that he proceed in a certain way if the long life of the patient is acknowledged as a desirable end. The application of anatomy, physiology, and pathology may just as well be used for the opposite end of killing a man. Whether it is wise to work toward long life, or whether it is better to kill people, is again a problem which lies outside the sphere of the applied sciences. Ethics or social philosophy or religion have to solve these preliminary questions. The physician as such has only to deal with the means which lead toward that goal.

We must make the same discrimination in the psychotechnical field. The psychologist may point out the methods by which an involuntary confession can be secured from a defendant, but whether it is justifiable to extort involuntary confessions is a problem which does not concern the psychologist. The lawyers or the legislators must decide as to the right or wrong, the legality or illegality, of forcing a man to show his hidden ideas. If such an end is desirable, the psychotechnical student can determine the right means, and that is the limit of his office. We ought to keep in mind that the same holds true for the application of psychology in economic life. Economic psychotechnics may serve certain ends of commerce and industry, but whether these ends are the best ones is not a care with which the psychologist has to be burdened. For instance, the end may be the selection of the most efficient laborers for particular industries. The psychologist may develop methods in his laboratory by which this purpose can be fulfilled. But if some mills prefer another goal, — for instance, to have not the most efficient but the cheapest possible laborers, — entirely different means for the selection are necessary. The psychologist is, therefore, not entangled in the economic discussions of the day; it is not his concern to decide whether the policy of the trusts or the policy of the trade-unions or any other policy for the selection of laborers is the ideal one. He is confined to the statement: if you wish this end, then you must proceed in this way; but it is left to you to express your preference among the ends. Applied psychology can, therefore, speak the language of an exact science in its own field, independent of economic opinions and debatable partisan interests. This is a necessary limitation, but in this limitation lies the strength of the new science. The psychologist may show how a special commodity can be advertised; but whether from a social point of view it is desirable to reinforce the sale of these goods is no problem for psychotechnics. If a sociologist insists that it would be better if not so many useless goods were bought, and that the aim ought rather to be to protect the buyer than to help the seller, the psychologist would not object. His interest would only be to find the right psychological means to lead to this other social end. He is partisan neither of the salesman nor of the customer, neither of the capitalist nor of the laborer, he is neither Socialist nor anti-Socialist, neither high-tariff man nor free-trader. Here, too, of course, there are certain goals which are acknowledged on all sides, and which therefore hardly need any discussion, just as in the case of the physician, where the prolongation of life is practically acknowledged as a desirable end by every one. But everywhere where the aim is not perfectly a matter of course, the psychotechnical specialist fulfills his task only when he is satisfied with demonstrating that certain psychical means serve a certain end, and that they ought to be applied as soon as that end is accepted.

The whole system of psychotechnical knowledge might be subdivided under either of the two aspects. Either we might start from the various mental processes and ask for what end each mental factor can be practically useful and important, or we can begin with studying what significant ends are acknowledged in our society and then we can seek the various psychological facts which are needed as means for the realization of these ends. The first way offers many conveniences. There we should begin with the mental states of attention, memory, feeling, and so on, and should study how the psychological knowledge of every one of these mental states can render service in many different practical fields. The attention, for instance, is important in the classroom when the teacher tries to secure the attention of the pupils, but the judge expects the same attention from the jurymen in the courtroom, the artist seeks to stir up the attention of the spectator, the advertiser demands the attention of the newspaper readers. Whoever studies the characteristics of the mental process of attention may then be able to indicate how in every one of these unlike cases the attention can be stimulated and retained. Nevertheless the opposite way which starts from the tasks to be fulfilled seems more helpful and more fundamentally significant. The question, then, is what mental processes become important for the tasks of education, what for the purposes of the courtroom, what for the hospital, what for the church, what for politics, and so on.

As this whole essay is to be devoted exclusively to the economic problems, we are obliged to choose the second way; that is, to arrange applied psychology with reference to its chief ends and not with reference to the various means. But the same question comes up in the further subdivision of the material. In the field of economic psychology, too, we might ask how far the study of attention, or of perception, or of feeling, or of will, or of memory, and so on, can be useful for the purposes of the business man. Or here, too, we might begin with the consideration of the various ends and purposes. The ends of commerce are different from those of industry, those of publishing different from those of transportation, those of agriculture different from those of mining; or, in the field of commerce, the purposes of the retailer are different from those of the wholesale merchant. There can be no limit to such subdivisions; each particular industry has its own aims, and in the same industry a large variety of tasks are united. We should accordingly be led to an ample classi-

fication of special economic ends with pigeonholes
for every possible kind of business and of labor.
The psychologist would have to find for every one
of these ends the right mental means. This would
be the ideal system of economic psychology.

But we are still endlessly far from such a perfect system. Modern educational psychology and
medical psychology have reached a stage at which
an effort for such a complete system might be
realized, but economic psychology is still at too
early a stage of development. It would be entirely
artificial to-day to aim at such ideal completeness.
If we were to construct such a complete system
of questions, we should have no answers. In the
present stage nothing can be seriously proposed
but the selection of a few central purposes which
occur in every department of business life, and a
study of the means to reach these special ends by
the discussion of some typical cases which may
clearly illustrate the methods involved.

From this point of view we select three chief
purposes of business life, purposes which are important in commerce and industry and every economic endeavor. We ask how we can find the
men whose mental qualities make them best fitted for the work which they have to do; secondly,
under what psychological conditions we can secure the greatest and most satisfactory output

INTRODUCTION

of work from every man; and finally, how we can produce most completely the influences on human minds which are desired in the interest of business. In other words, we ask how to find the best possible man, how to produce the best possible work, and how to secure the best possible effects.

PART I

THE BEST POSSIBLE MAN

PART I

THE BEST POSSIBLE MAN

IV

VOCATION AND FITNESS

INSTEAD of lingering over theoretical discussions, we will move straight on toward our first practical problem. The economic task, with reference to which we want to demonstrate the new psychotechnic method, is the selection of those personalities which by their mental qualities are especially fit for a particular kind of economic work. This problem is especially useful to show what the new method can do and what it cannot do. Whether the method is sufficiently developed to secure full results to-day, or whether they will come to-morrow, is unimportant. It is clear that the success of to-morrow is to be hoped for, only if understanding and interest in the problem is already alive to-day.

When we inquire into the qualities of men, we use the word here in its widest meaning. It covers, on the one side, the mental dispositions which may still be quite undeveloped and which may unfold only under the influence of special conditions in the surroundings; but, on the other side, it covers the habitual traits of the personality, the features of the individual temperament and character, of the intelligence and of the ability, of the collected knowledge and of the acquired experience. All variations of will and feeling, of perception and thought, of attention and emotion, of memory and imagination, are included here. From a purely psychological standpoint, quite incomparable contents and functions and dispositions of the personality are thus thrown together, but in practical life we are accustomed to proceed after this fashion: If a man applies for a position, he is considered with regard to the totality of his qualities, and at first nobody cares whether the particular feature is inherited or acquired, whether it is an individual chance variation or whether it is common to a larger group, perhaps to all members of a certain nationality or race. We simply start from the clear fact that the personalities which enter into the world of affairs present an unlimited manifoldness of talents and abilities and functions of the mind. From this manifoldness, it necessarily follows that some are more, some less, fit for the particular economic task. In view of the far-reaching division of labor in our modern economic life, it is impossible to avoid the ques-

tion how we can select the fit personalities and re-
ject the unfit ones.

How has modern society prepared itself to
settle this social demand? In case that certain
knowledge is indispensable for the work or that
technical abilities must have been acquired, the
vocation is surrounded by examinations. This is
true of the lower as well as of the higher activities. The direct examination is everywhere supplemented by testimonials covering the previous
achievements, by certificates referring to the
previous education, and in frequent cases by the
endeavor to gain a personal impression from
the applicant. But if we take all this together,
the total result remains a social machinery by
which perhaps the elimination of the entirely unfit can be secured. But no one could speak of a
really satisfactory adaptation of the manifold personalities to the economic vocational tasks. All
those examinations and tests and certificates refer essentially to what can be learned from without, and not to the true qualities of the mind and
the deeper traits. The so-called impressions, too,
are determined by the most secondary and external factors. Society relies instinctively on the hope
that the natural wishes and interests will push
every one to the place for which his dispositions,
talents, and psychophysical gifts prepare him.

THE BEST POSSIBLE MAN

In reality this confidence is entirely unfounded. A threefold difficulty exists. In the first place, young people know very little about themselves and their abilities. When the day comes on which they discover their real strong points and their weaknesses, it is often too late. They have usually been drawn into the current of a particular vocation, and have given too much energy to the preparation for a specific achievement to change the whole life-plan once more. The entire scheme of education gives to the individual little chance to find himself. A mere interest for one or another subject in school is influenced by many accidental circumstances, by the personality of the teacher or the methods of instruction, by suggestions of the surroundings and by home traditions, and accordingly even such a preference gives rather a slight final indication of the individual mental qualities. Moreover, such mere inclinations and interests cannot determine the true psychological fitness for a vocation. To choose a crude illustration, a boy may think with passion of the vocation of a sailor, and yet may be entirely unfit for it, because his mind lacks the ability to discriminate red and green. He himself may never have discovered that he is color-blind, but when he is ready to turn to the sailor's calling, the examination of his color-sensitiveness which is demanded

30

may have shown the disturbing mental deficiency. Similar defects may exist in a boy's attention or memory, judgment or feeling, thought or imagination, suggestibility or emotion, and they may remain just as undiscovered as the defect of color-blindness, which is characteristic of four per cent of the male population. All such deficiencies may be dangerous in particular callings. But while the vocation of the ship officer is fortunately protected nowadays by such a special psychological examination, most other vocations are unguarded against the entrance of the mentally unfit individuals.

As the boys and girls grow up without recognizing their psychical weaknesses, the exceptional strength of one or another mental function too often remains unnoticed by them as well. They may find out when they are favored with a special talent for art or music or scholarship, but they hardly ever know that their attention, or their memory, or their will, or their intellectual apprehension, or their sensory perceptions, are unusually developed in a particular direction; yet such an exceptional mental disposition might be the cause of special success in certain vocations. But we may abstract from the extremes of abnormal deficiency and abnormal overdevelopment in particular functions. Between them we find the

broad region of the average minds with their numberless variations, and these variations are usually
quite unknown to their possessors. It is often
surprising to see how the most manifest differences of psychical organization remain unnoticed
by the individuals themselves. Men with a pronounced visual type of memory and men with a
marked acoustical type may live together without
the slightest idea that their contents of consciousness are fundamentally different from each other.
Neither the children nor their parents nor their
teachers burden themselves with the careful
analysis of such actual mental qualities when the
choice of a vocation is before them. They know
that a boy who is completely unmusical must not
become a musician, and that the child who cannot
draw at all must not become a painter, just as on
physical grounds a boy with very weak muscles
is not fit to become a blacksmith. But as soon
as the subtler differentiation is needed, the judgment of all concerned seems helpless and the
psychical characteristics remain disregarded.

A further reason for the lack of adaptation, and
surely a most important one, lies in the fact that
the individual usually knows only the most external conditions of the vocations from which he
chooses. The most essential requisite for a truly
perfect adaptation, namely, a real analysis of the

vocational demands with reference to the desirable personal qualities, is so far not in existence. The young people generally see some superficial traits of the careers which seem to stand open, and, besides, perhaps they notice the great rewards of the most successful. The inner labor, the inner values, and the inner difficulties and frictions are too often unknown to those who decide for a vocation, and they are unable to correlate those essential factors of the life-calling with all that nature by inheritance, and society by surroundings and training, have planted and developed in their minds.

In addition to this ignorance as to one's own mental disposition and to the lack of understanding of the true mental requirements of the various social tasks comes finally the abundance of trivial chance influences which become decisive in the choice of a vocation. Vocation and marriage are the two most consequential decisions in life. In the selection of a husband or wife, too, the decision is very frequently made dependent upon the most superficial and trivial motives. Yet the social philosopher may content himself with the belief that even in the fugitive love desire a deeper instinct of nature is expressed, which may at least serve the biological tasks of married life. In the choice of a vocation, even such a belief in a bio-

logical instinct is impossible. The choice of a vocation, determined by fugitive whims and chance
fancies, by mere imitation, by a hope for quick
earnings, by irresponsible recommendation, or by
mere laziness, has no internal reason or excuse.
Illusory ideas as to the prospects of a career,
moreover, often falsify the whole vista; and if we
consider all this, we can hardly be surprised that
our total result is in many respects hardly better
than if everything were left entirely to accident.
Even on the height of a mental training to the
end of adolescence, we see how the college grad-
uates are too often led by accidental motives to
the decision whether they shall become lawyers or
physicians or business men, but this superficiality
of choice of course appears much more strongly
where the lifework is to be built upon the basis
of a mere elementary or high school education.

The final result corresponds exactly to these
conditions. Everywhere, in all countries and in
all vocations, but especially in the economic careers, we hear the complaint that there is lack of
really good men. Everywhere places are waiting
for the right man, while at the same time we find
everywhere an oversupply of mediocre aspirants.
This, however, does not in the least imply that
there really are not enough personalities who might
be perfectly fit even for the highest demands of

the vocations; it means only that as a matter of course the result in the filling of positions cannot be satisfactory, if the placing of the individuals is carried on without serious regard for the personal mental qualities. The complaint that there is lack of fit human material would probably never entirely disappear, as with a better adjustment of the material, the demands would steadily increase; but it could at least be predicted with high probability that this lack of really fit material would not be felt so keenly everywhere if the really decisive factor for the adjustment of personality and vocation, namely, the dispositions of the mind, were not so carelessly ignored.

Society, to be sure, has a convenient means of correction. The individual tries, and when he is doing his work too badly, he loses his job, he is pushed out from the career which he has chosen, with the great probability that he will be crushed by the wheels of social life. It is a rare occurrence for the man who is a failure in his chosen vocation, and who has been thrown out of it, to happen to come into the career in which he can make a success. Social statistics show with an appalling clearness what a burden and what a danger to the social body is growing from the masses of those who do not succeed and who by their lack of success become discouraged and embittered. The social psychologist cannot resist the conviction that every single one could have found a place in which he could have achieved something of value for the commonwealth. The laborer, who in spite of his best efforts shows himself useless and clumsy before one machine, might perhaps have done satisfactory work in the next mill where the machines demand another type of mental reaction. His psychical rhythm and his inner functions would be able to adjust themselves to the requirements of the one kind of labor and not to those of the other. Truly the whole social body has had to pay a heavy penalty for not making even the faintest effort to settle systematically the fundamental problem of vocational choice, the problem of the psychical adaptation of the individuality. An improvement would lie equally in the interest of those who seek positions and those who have positions to offer. The employers can hope that in all departments better work will be done as soon as better adapted individuals can be obtained; and, on the other hand, those who are anxious to make their working energies effective may expect that the careful selection of individual mental characters for the various tasks of the world will insure not only greater success and gain, but above all greater joy in the work, deeper satisfaction, and more harmonious unfolding of the personality.

V

OBSERVATIONS of this kind, which refer to the borderland region between psychology and social politics, are valid for all modern nations. Yet it is hardly a chance that the first efforts toward a systematic overcoming of some of these difficulties have been made with us in America. The barriers between the classes lie lower; here the choice of a vocation is less determined by tradition; and it belongs to the creed of political democracy that just as everybody can be called to the highest elective offices, so everybody ought to be fit for any vocation in any sphere of life. The wandering from calling to calling is more frequent in America than anywhere else. To be sure, this has the advantage that a failure in one vocation does not bring with it such a serious injury as in Europe, but it contributes much to the greater danger that any one may jump recklessly and without preparation into any vocational stream.

It is fresh in every one's mind how during the last decade the economic conscience of the whole American nation became aroused. Up to the end

37

of the last century the people had lived with the secure feeling of possessing a country with inexhaustible treasures. The last few years brought the reaction, and it became increasingly clear how irresponsible the national attitude had been, how the richness of the forests and the mines and the rivers had been recklessly squandered without any thought of the future. Conservation of the national possessions suddenly became the battle-cry, and this turned the eye also to that limitless waste of human material, a waste going on everywhere in the world, but nowhere more widely than in the United States. The feeling grew that no waste of valuable possessions is so reckless as that which results from the distributing of living force by chance methods instead of examining carefully how work and workmen can fit one another. While this was the emotional background, two significant social movements originated in our midst. The two movements were entirely independent of each other, but from two different starting-points they worked in one respect toward the same goal. They are social and economic movements, neither of which at first had anything directly to do with psychological questions; but both led to a point where the psychological turn of the problem seemed unavoidable. Here begins the obligation of the psychologist, and the possibility of fulfilling this obligation will be the topic of our discussion concerning the selection of the best man.

These two American movements which we have in mind are the effort to furnish to pupils leaving the school guidance in their choice of a vocation, and the nowadays still better known movement toward scientific management in commerce and industry. The movement toward vocational guidance is externally still rather modest and confined to very narrow circles, but it is rapidly spreading and is not without significant achievements. It started in Boston. There the late Mr. Parsons once called a meeting of all the boys of his neighborhood who were to leave the elementary schools at the end of the year. He wanted to consider with them whether they had reasonable plans for their future. At the well-attended meeting it became clear that the boys knew little concerning what they had to expect in practical life, and Parsons was able to give them, especially in individual discussions, much helpful information. They knew too little of the characteristic features of the vocations to which they wanted to devote themselves, and they had given hardly any attention to the question whether they had the necessary qualifications for the special work. From this germ grew a little office which was

opened in 1908, in which all Boston boys and girls
at the time when they left school were to receive
individual suggestions with reference to the most
reasonable and best adjusted selection of a calling.
There is hardly any doubt that the remarkable
success of this modest beginning was dependent
upon the admirable personality of the late or-
ganizer, who recognized the individual features
with unusual tact and acumen. But he himself
had no doubt that such a merely impressionistic
method could not satisfy the demands. He saw
that a threefold advance would become necessary.
First, it was essential to analyze the objective
relations of the many hundred kinds of accessible
vocations. Their economic, hygienic, technical,
and social elements ought to be examined so that
every boy and girl could receive reliable information as to the demands of the vocation and as to
the prospects and opportunities in it. Secondly,
it would become essential to interest the schools
in all these complex questions of vocational
choice, so that, by observation of individual tendencies and abilities of the pupils, the teachers
might furnish preparatory material for the work
of the institute for vocational guidance. Thirdly,
— and this is for us the most important point, —
he saw that the methods had to be elaborated in
such a way that the personal traits and disposi-

tions might be discovered with much greater exactitude and with much richer detail than was possible through what a mere call on the vocational counselor could unveil.[3]

It is well known how this Boston bureau has stimulated a number of American cities to come forward with similar beginnings. The pedagogical circles have been especially aroused by the movement, municipal and philanthropic boards have at least approached this group of problems, two important conferences for vocational guidance have met in New York, and at various places the question has been discussed whether or not a vocational counselor might be attached to the schools in a position similar to that of the school physician. The chief progress has been made in the direction of collecting reliable data with reference to the economic and hygienic conditions of the various vocations, the demand and supply and the scale of wages. In short, everything connected with the externalities of the vocations has been carefully analyzed, and sufficient reliable material has been gained, at least regarding certain local conditions. In the place of individual advice, we have thus to a certain degree obtained general economic investigations from which each can gather what he needs. It seems that sometimes the danger of letting such offices degenerate into mere agencies for employment has not been avoided, but that is one of the perils of the first development. The mother institute in Boston, too, under its new direction emphasizes more the economic and hygienic side, and has set its centre of gravity in a systematic effort to propagate understanding of the problems of vocational guidance and to train professional vocational counselors in systematic courses, who are then to carry the interest over the land.[4]

The real psychological analysis with which the movement began has, therefore, been somewhat pushed aside for a while, and the officers of those institutes declare frankly that they want to return to the mental problem only after professional psychologists have sufficiently worked out the specific methods for its mastery. Most counselors seem to feel instinctively that the core of the whole matter lies in the psychological examination. but they all agree that for this they must wait until the psychological laboratories can furnish them with really reliable means and schemes. Certainly it is very important, for instance, that boys with weak lungs be kept away from such industrial vocations as have been shown by the statistics to be dangerous for the lungs, or that the onrush to vocations be stopped where the statistics allow it to be foreseen that there will soon be an oversupply of workers. But, after all, it remains much more decisive for the welfare of the community, and for the future life happiness of those who leave the school, that every one turn to those forms of work to which his psychological traits are adjusted, or at least that he be kept away from those in which his mental qualities and dispositions would make a truly successful advance improbable.

The problem accordingly has been handed over from the vocational counselors to the experimental psychologists, and it is certainly in the spirit of the modern tendency toward applied psychology that the psychological laboratories undertake the investigation and withdraw it from the dilettantic discussion of amateur psychologists or the mere impressionism of the school-teachers. Even those early beginnings indicate clearly that the goal can be reached only through exact, scientific, experimental research, and that the mere naïve methods — for instance, the filling-out of questionnaires which may be quite useful in the first approach — cannot be sufficient for a real, persistent furtherance of economic life and of the masses who seek their vocations. In order to gain an analysis of the individual, Parsons made every applicant answer in writing a long series of questions which referred to his habits and his emotions, his inclinations and his expectations, his traits and his experiences. The psychologist, however, can hardly be in doubt that just the mental qualities which ought to be most important for the vocational counselor can scarcely be found out by such methods. We have emphasized before that the ordinary individual knows very little of his own mental functions: on the whole, he knows them as little as he knows the muscles which he uses when he talks or walks. Among his questions Parsons included such ones as: "Are your manners quiet, noisy, boisterous, deferential, or self-assertive? Are you thoughtful of the comfort of others? Do you smile naturally and easily, or is your face ordinarily expressionless? Are you frank, kindly, cordial, respectful, courteous in word and actions? Do you look people frankly in the eye? Are your inflections natural, courteous, modest, musical, or aggressive, conceited, pessimistic, repellent? What are your powers of attention, observation, memory, reason, imagination, inventiveness, thoughtfulness, receptiveness, quickness, analytical power, constructiveness, breadth, grasp? Can you manage people well? Do you know a fine picture when you see it? Is your will weak, yielding, vacillating, or firm, strong, stubborn? Do you like to be with people and do they like to be with you?" — and so on. It is clear that the replies to questions of this kind can be of psychological value only when the questioner knows beforehand the mind of the youth, and can accordingly judge with what degree of understanding, sincerity, and ability the circular blanks have been filled out. But as the questions are put for the very purpose of revealing the personality, the entire effort tends to move in a circle.

To break this circle, it indeed becomes necessary to emancipate one's self from the method of ordinary self-observation and to replace it by objective experiment in the psychological laboratory. Experimentation in such a laboratory stands in no contrast to the method of introspection. A contrast does exist between self-observation and observation on children or patients or primitive peoples or animals. In their case the psychologist observes his material from without. But in the case of the typical laboratory experiment, everything is ultimately based on self-observation; only we have to do with the self-observation under exact conditions which the experimenter is able to control and to vary at will. Even Parsons sometimes turned to little experimental inquiries in which he simplified some well-known methods of the laboratory in order to secure with the most elementary means a certain objective foundation for his mental analysis. For instance, he sometimes examined the memory by reading to the boys graded sentences containing from ten to fifty words and having them repeat what they remembered, or he measured with a watch the rapidity of reading and writing, or he determined the sensitiveness for the discrimination of differences by asking them to make a point with a pencil in the centres of circles of various sizes. But if such experimental schemes, even of the simplest form, are in question, it seems a matter of course that the plan ought to be prescribed by real scientists who specialize in the psychological field. The psychologist, for instance, surely cannot agree to a method which measures the memory by such a method of having spoken sentences repeated and the quality of the memory faculty naïvely graded according to the results. He knows too well that there are many different kinds of memory, and would always determine first which type of memory functions is to be examined if memory achievements are needed for a particular calling.

But even with a more exact method of experimenting, such a procedure would not be sufficient to solve the true problem. A second step would still be necessary: namely, the adaptation of the experimental result to the special psychological requirements of the economic activity; and this again presupposes an independent psychological analysis. Most of the previous efforts have suffered from the carelessness with which this second step was ignored, and the special mental requirements were treated as a matter of course upon which any layman could judge. In reality they need the most careful psychological analysis, and only if this is carried out with the means of scientific psychology, can a study of the abilities of the individual become serviceable to the demands of the market. Such a psychological disentangling of the requirements of the callings, in the interest of guidance, is attempted in the material which the various vocational institutes have prepared, but it seldom goes beyond commonplaces. We read there, for instance,[5] for the confectioner: "Boys in this industry must be clean, quick, and strong. The most important qualities desired are neatness and adaptability to routine"; or for the future baker, the boy "ought to know how to conduct himself and to meet the public"; or for the future architectural designer, "he must have creative ability, artistic feeling, and power to sketch"; or for the dressmaker, she "should have good eyesight and good sense of color, and an ability to use her hands readily; she should be able to apply herself steadily and be fairly quick in her movements; neatness of person is also essential"; or for the stenographer, she must be "possessed of intelligence, good judgment, and common sense; must have good eyesight, good hearing, and a good memory; must have quick perception, and be able to concentrate her attention completely on any matter in hand." It is evident that all this is extremely far from any psychological analysis in the terms of science. All taken together, we may, therefore, say that in the movement for vocational guidance practically nothing has been done to make modern experimental psychology serviceable to the new task. But on the one side, it has shown that this work of the experimental psychologist is the next step necessary. On the other side, it has become evident that in the vocation bureaus appropriate social agencies are existing which are ready to take up the results of such work, and to apply them for the good of the American youth and of commerce and industry, as soon as the experimental psychologist has developed the significant methods.

VI

B EFORE we discuss some cases of such experimental investigations, we may glance at that other American movement, the well-known systematic effort toward scientific management which has often been interpreted in an expansive literature.[6] Enthusiastic followers have declared it to be the greatest advance in industry since the introduction of the mill system and of machinery. Opponents have hastily denounced it as a mistake, and have insisted that it proved a failure in the factories in which it has been introduced. A sober examination of the facts soon demonstrates that the truth lies in the middle. Those followers of Frederick W. Taylor who have made almost a religion out of his ideas have certainly often exaggerated the practical applicability of the new theories, and their actual reforms in the mills have not seldom shown that the system is still too topheavy; that is, there are too many higher employees necessary in order to keep the works running on principles of scientific management. On the other hand, the opposition which comes from certain quarters, — for instance, from some trade-unions, — may be disregarded, as it is not directed against the claim that the efficiency can be heightened, but only against some social features of the scheme, such as the resulting temporary reduction of the number of workmen. But nobody can deny that this revolutionary movement has introduced most valuable suggestions which the industrial world cannot afford to ignore, and that as soon as exaggerations are avoided and experience has created a broader foundation, the principles of the new theory will prove of lasting value. We shall have to discuss, at a later point, various special features of the system, especially the highly interesting motion study. Here we have to deal only with those tendencies of the movement and with those interests which point toward our present problem, the mental analysis of the individual employees in order to avoid misfits.

The approach to this problem, indeed, seems unavoidable for the students of scientific management, as its goal is an organization of economic work by which the waste of energy will be avoided and the greatest increase in the efficiency of the industrial enterprise will be reached. The recognition that this can never be effected by a mere excessive driving of the workingmen belongs to its very presuppositions. The illusory means of

prolongation of the working-time and similar devices by which the situation of the individual de-
teriorates would be out of the question; on the
contrary, the heightening of the individual's joy
in the work and of the personal satisfaction in
one's total life development belongs among the
most important indirect agencies of the new
scheme. This end is reached by many characteristic changes in the division of labor; also by a
new division between supervisors and workers, by
transformations of the work itself and of the tools
and vehicles. But as a by-product of these efforts
the demand necessarily arose for means by which
the fit individuals could be found for special kinds
of labor. The more scientific management introduced changes by which the individual achievement often had to become rather complicated and
difficult, the more it became necessary to study
the skill and the endurance and the intelligence
of the individual laborers in order to entrust these
new difficult tasks only to the most appropriate
men in the factories and mills. The problem of
individual selection accordingly forced itself on
the new efficiency engineers, and they naturally
recognized that the really essential traits and dispositions were the mental ones. In the most progressive books of the new movement, this need of
emphasizing the selection of workers with refer-

ence to their mental equipment comes to clear expression.

Yet this is very far from a real application of scientific psychology to the problem at hand. Wherever the question of the selection of the fit men after psychological principles is mentioned in the literature of this movement, the language becomes vague, and the same men, who use the newest scientific knowledge whenever physics or mathematics or physiology or chemistry are involved, make hardly any attempts to introduce the results of science when psychology is in question. The clearest insight into the general situation may be found in the most recent books by Emerson. He says frankly: "It is psychology, not soil or climate, that enables a man to raise five times as many potatoes per acre as the average in his own state"; [7] or: "In selecting human assistants such superficialities as education, as physical strength, even antecedent morality, are not as important as the inner attitudes, proclivities, character, which after all determine the man or woman." [8] He also fully recognizes the necessity of securing as early as possible the psychological essentials. He says: "The type for the great newspaper is set up by linotype operators. Apprenticeship is rigorously limited. Some operators can never get beyond the 2500-em class, others with no more personal effort can set 5000 ems. Do the employers test out applicants for apprenticeship so as to be sure to secure boys who will develop into the 5000-em class? They do not: they select applicants for any near reason except the fundamental important one of innate fitness." [9] But all this points only to the existence of the problem, and in reality gives not even a hint for its solution. The theorists of scientific management seem to think that the most subtle methods are indispensable for physical measurements, but for psychological inquiry nothing but a kind of intuition is necessary. Emerson tells how, for instance, "The competent specialist who has supplemented natural gifts and good judgment by analysis and synthesis can perceive attitudes and proclivities even in the very young, much more readily in those semi-matured, and can with almost infallible certainty point out, not only what work can be undertaken with fair hope of success, but also what slight modification or addition and diminution will more than double the personal power." [10] The true psychological specialists surely ought to decline this flattering confidence. Far from the "almost infallible certainty," they can hardly expect even a moderate amount of success in such directions so long as specific methods have not been elaborated, and so long as no way has

been shown to make experimental measurements
by which such mere guesswork can be replaced
by scientific investigation.

The only modest effort to try a step in this
direction toward the psychological laboratory is
recorded by Taylor,[11] who tells of Mr. S. E.
Thompson's work in a bicycle ball factory, where
a hundred and twenty girls were inspecting the
balls. They had to place a row of small polished
steel balls on the back of the left hand and while
they were rolled over and over in the crease between two of the fingers placed together, they
were minutely examined in a strong light and the
defective balls were picked out with the aid of a
magnet held in the right hand. The work required the closest attention and concentration.
The girls were working ten and a half hours a day.
Mr. Thompson soon recognized that the quality
most needed, beside endurance and industry, was
a quick power of perception accompanied by
quick responsive action. He knew that the psychological laboratory has developed methods for
a very exact measurement of the time needed to
react on an impression with the quickest possible
movement; it is called the reaction-time, and is
usually measured in thousandths of a second. He
therefore considered it advisable to measure the
reaction-time of the girls, and to eliminate from

service all those who showed a relatively long time between the stimulus and reaction. This involved laying off many of the most intelligent, hardest-working, and most trustworthy girls. Yet the effect was the possibility of shortening the hours and of reducing more and more the number of workers, with the final outcome that thirty-five girls did the work formerly done by a hundred and twenty, and that the accuracy of the work at the higher speed was two thirds greater than at the former slow speed. This allowed almost a doubling of the wages of the girls in spite of their shorter working-day, and at the same time a considerable reduction in the cost of the work for the factory. This excursion of an efficiency engineer into the psychological laboratory remained, however, an entirely exceptional case. Moreover, such a reaction-time measurement did not demand any special development of new methods or any particular mental analysis, and this exception thus confirms the rule that the followers of scientific management principles have recognized the need of psychological inquiries, but have not done anything worth mentioning to apply the results of really scientific psychology. Hence the situation is the same as in the field of vocational guidance. In both cases a vague longing for psychological analysis and psychological measurement, but in both cases so far everything has remained on the level of helpless psychological dilettantism. It stands in striking contrast with the scientific seriousness with which the economic questions are taken up in the field of vocational guidance and the physical questions in the field of scientific management. It is, therefore, evidently the duty of the experimental psychologists themselves to examine the ground from the point of view of the psychological laboratory.

VII

THE METHODS OF EXPERIMENTAL PSYCHOLOGY

WE now see clearly the psychotechnical problem. We have to analyze definite economic tasks with reference to the mental qualities which are necessary or desirable for them, and we have to find methods by which these mental qualities can be tested. We must, indeed, insist on it that the interests of commerce and industry can be helped only when both sides, the vocational demands and the personal function, are examined with equal scientific thoroughness. One aspect alone is unsatisfactory. It would of course be possible to confine the examination to the individual mental traits, and then theoretically to determine for which economic tasks the presence of these qualities would be useful and for which tasks their absence or their deficiency would be fatal. Common sense may be sufficient to lead us a few steps in that direction. For instance, if we find by psychological examination that an individual is color-blind for red and green sensations, we may at once conclude, without any real psychological analysis of the vocations, that he would be unfit for the railroad service or the naval service, in which red and green signals are of importance. We may also decide at once that such a boy would be useless for all artistic work in which the nuances of colors are of consequence, or as a laborer in certain departments of a dyeing establishment, and that such a color-blind girl would not do at a dressmaker's or in a millinery store. But if we come to the question whether such a color-blind individual may enter into the business of gardening, in spite of the inability to distinguish the strawberries in the bed or the red flowers among the green leaves, the first necessity, after all, would be to find out how far the particular demands of this vocation make the ability to discriminate color a prerequisite, and how far psychical substitutions, such as a recognition of the forms and of differences in the light intensity, may be sufficient for the practical task. Moreover, where not merely such mental defects, but more subtly shaded variations within normal limits are involved, it would be superficial, if only the mental states were examined and not at the same time the mental requirements of the vocations themselves. The vocation should rather remain the starting-point. We must at first find out what demands on the mental system are made by it, and we must grade these demands in order to recognize the more or less important ones, and, especially for the important ones, we must then seek exact standards with experimental methods.

Such an experimental investigation may proceed according to either of two different principles. One way is to take the mental process which is demanded by the industrial work as an undivided whole. In this case we have to construct experimental conditions under which this total activity can be performed in a gradual, measurable way. The psychical part of the vocational work thus becomes schematized, and is simply rendered experimentally on a reduced scale. The other way is to resolve the mental process into its components and to test every single elementary function in its isolated form. In this latter case the examination has the advantage of having at its disposal all the familiar methods of experimental psychology, while in the first case for every special vocational situation perfectly new experimental tests must be devised.

Whether the one or the other method is to be preferred must depend upon the nature of the particular commercial or industrial calling, and accordingly presupposes a careful analysis of the special economical processes. It is, indeed, easy to recognize that in certain industrial activities a series of psychical functions is in question which all lie side by side and which do not fuse into one united total process, however much they may influence one another. But for many industrial tasks just this unity is the essential condition. The testing of the mental elements would be in such cases as insufficient as if we were to test a machine with reference to its parts only and not with reference to its total united performance. Even in this latter case this unified function does not represent the total personality: it is always merely a segment of the whole mental life. We may examine with psychological methods, for instance, the fitness of an employee for a technical vocation and may test the particular complex unified combination of attention, imagination and intelligence, will and memory, which is essential for that special kind of labor. We may be able to reconstruct the conditions so completely that we would feel justified in predicting whether the individual can fulfill that technical task or not; and yet we may disregard entirely the question whether that man is honest or dishonest, whether he is pacific or quarrelsome; in short, whether his mental disposition makes him a desirable member of that industrial concern under other aspects.

We best recognize the significance of these various methods by selecting a few concrete cases as illustrations and analzying them in detail. But a word of warning may be given beforehand so as to avoid misunderstandings. These examples do not stand here as reports of completed investigations, the results of which ought to be accepted as conclusive parts of the new psychotechnical science; they are not presented as if the results were to be recommended like a well-tested machine for practical purposes. Such really completed investigations do not as yet exist in this field. All that can be offered is modest pioneer work, and just these inquiries into the mental qualities and their relations to the industrial vocations have attracted my attention only very recently, and therefore certainly still demand long continuations of the experiments in ēvery direction. But we may hope for satisfactory results the earlier, the more coöperators are entering the field, and the more such researches are started in other places and in other institutions. I therefore offer these early reports at the first stage of my research merely as stimulations, so as to demonstrate the possibilities.

As an illustration of the method of examining the mental process as a whole, I propose to discuss the case of the motormen in the electric railways. As an illustration of the other type, namely, of analyzing the activity and testing the elementary functions, I shall discuss the case of the employees in the telephone service. I select these two functions, as both play a practically important rôle in the technique of modern economic life and as in both occupations very large numbers of individuals are engaged in the work.

VIII

EXPERIMENTS IN THE INTEREST OF ELECTRIC RAILWAY SERVICE

THE problem of securing fit motormen for the electric railways was brought to my attention from without. The accidents which occurred through the fault, or at least not without the fault, of the motormen in street railway transportation have always aroused disquietude and even indignation in the public, and the street railway companies suffered much from the many payments of indemnity imposed by the court as they amounted to thirteen per cent of the gross earnings of some companies. Last winter the American Association for Labor Legislation called a meeting of vocational specialists to discuss the problem of these accidents under various aspects. The street railways of various cities were represented, and economic, physiological, and psychological specialists took part in the general discussion. Much attention was given, of course, to the questions of fatigue and to the statistical results as to the number of accidents and their relation to the various hours of the day and to the time of labor. But there was a strong tendency to recognize, as still more important than the mere fatigue, the whole mental constitution of the motormen. The ability to keep attention constant, to resist distraction by chance happenings on the street, and especially the always needed ability to foresee the possible movements of the pedestrians and vehicles were acknowledged as extremely different from man to man. The companies claimed that there are motormen who practically never have an accident, because they feel beforehand even what the confused pedestrian and the unskilled chauffeur will do, while others relatively often experience accidents of all kinds because they do not foresee how matters will develop. They can hardly be blamed, as they were not careless, and yet the accidents did result from their personal qualities; they simply lacked the gift of instinctive foresight. All this turned the attention more and more to the possibilities of psychological analysis, and the Association suggested that I undertake an inquiry into this interesting problem with the means of the psychological laboratory. I felt the practical importance of the problem, considering that there are electric railway companies in this country which have up to fifty thousand accident indemnity cases a year. It therefore seemed to me decidedly worth while to undertake a laboratory investigation.

ELECTRIC RAILWAY SERVICE

It would have been quite possible to treat the functions of the motormen according to the method which resolves the complex achievement into its various elements and tests every function independently. For instance, the stopping of the car as soon as the danger of an accident threatens is evidently effective only if the movement controlling the lever is carried out with sufficient rapidity. We should accordingly be justified in examining the quickness with which the individual reacts on optical stimuli. If a playing child suddenly runs across the track of the electric railway, a difference of a tenth of a second in the reaction-time may decide his fate. But I may say at once that I did not find characteristic differences in the rapidity of reaction of those motormen whom the company had found reliable and those who have frequent accidents. It seems that the slow individuals do not remain in the service at all. As a matter of course certain other indispensable single functions, like sharpness of vision, are examined before the entrance into the service and so they cannot stand as characteristic conditions of good or bad service among the actual employees.

For this reason, in the case of the motormen I abstracted from the study of single elementary functions and turned my attention to that mental process which after some careful observations seemed to me the really central one for the problem of accidents. I found this to be a particular complicated act of attention by which the manifoldness of objects, the pedestrians, the carriages, and the automobiles, are continuously observed with reference to their rapidity and direction in the quickly changing panorama of the street. Moving figures come from the right and from the left toward and across the track, and are embedded in a stream of men and vehicles which moves parallel to the track. In the face of such manifoldness there are men whose impulses are almost inhibited and who instinctively desire to wait for the movement of the nearest objects; they would evidently be unfit for the service, as they would drive the electric car far too slowly. There are others who, even with the car at high speed, can adjust themselves for a time to the complex moving situation, but whose attention soon lapses, and while they are fixating a rather distant carriage, may overlook a pedestrian who carelessly crosses the track immediately in front of their car. In short, we have a great variety of mental types of this characteristic unified activity, which may be understood as a particular combination of attention and imagination.

My effort was to transplant this activity of the motormen into laboratory processes. And here

ELECTRIC RAILWAY SERVICE

I may include a remark on the methodology of psychological industrial experiments. One might naturally think that the experience of a special industrial undertaking would be best reproduced for the experiment by repeating the external conditions in a kind of miniature form. That would mean that we ought to test the motormen of the electric railway by experiments with small toy models of electric cars placed on the laboratory table. But this would be decidedly inappropriate. A reduced copy of an external apparatus may arouse ideas, feelings, and volitions which have little in common with the processes of actual life. The presupposition would be that the man to be tested for any industrial achievement would have to think himself into the miniature situation, and especially uneducated persons are often very unsuccessful in such efforts. This can be clearly seen from the experiences before naval courts, where it is usual to demonstrate collisions of ships by small ship models on the table in the courtroom. Experience has frequently shown that helmsmen, who have found their course a life long among real vessels in the harbor and on the sea, become entirely confused when they are to demonstrate by the models the relative positions of the ships. Even in the naval war schools where the officers play at war with small model ships, a certain inner readjustment is always necessary for them to bring the miniature ships on the large table into the tactical game. On the water, for instance, the naval officer sees the far-distant ships very much smaller than those near by, while on the naval game table all the ships look equally large. On the whole, I feel inclined to say from my experience so far that experiments with small models of the actual industrial mechanism are hardly appropriate for investigations in the field of economic psychology. The essential point for the psychological experiment is not the external similarity of the apparatus, but exclusively the inner similarity of the mental attitude. The more the external mechanism with which or on which the action is carried out becomes schematized, the more the action itself will appear in its true character.

In the method of my experiments with the motormen, accordingly, I had to satisfy only two demands. The method of examination promised to be valuable if, first, it showed good results with reliable motormen and bad results with unreliable ones; and, secondly, if it vividly aroused in all the motormen the feeling that the mental function which they were going through during the experiment had the greatest possible similarity with their experience on the front platform of the electric car. These are the true tests of a desirable experimental method, while it is not necessary that the apparatus be similar to the electric car or that the external activities in the experiment be identical with their performance in the service. After several unsatisfactory efforts, in which I worked with too complicated instruments, I finally settled on the following arrangement of the experiment which seems to me to satisfy those two demands.

The street is represented by a card 9 half-inches broad and 26 half-inches long. Two heavy lines half an inch apart go lengthwise through the centre of the card, and accordingly a space of 4 half-inches remains on either side. The whole card is divided into small half-inch squares which we consider as the unit. Thus there is in any cross-section 1 unit between the two central lines and 4 units on either side. Lengthwise there are 26 units. The 26 squares which lie between the two heavy central lines are marked with the printed letters of the alphabet from A to Z. These two heavy central lines are to represent an electric railway track on a street. On either side the 4 rows of squares are filled in an irregular way with black and red figures of the three first digits. The digit 1 always represents a pedestrian who moves just one step, and that means from one unit into the next; the digit 2 a horse, which moves twice as fast, that is, which moves 2 units; and the digit 3 an automobile which moves three times as fast, that is, 3 units. Moreover, the black digits stand for men, horses, and automobiles which move parallel to the track and cannot cross the track, and are therefore to be disregarded in looking out for dangers. The red digits, on the other hand, are the dangerous ones. They move from either side toward the track. The idea is that the man to be experimented on is to find as quickly as possible those points on the track which are threatened by the red figures, that is, those letters in the 26 track units at which the red figures would land, if they make the steps which their number indicates. A red digit 3 which is 4 steps from the track is to be disregarded, because it would not reach the track. A red digit 3 which is only 1 or 2 steps from the track is also to be disregarded, because it would cross beyond the track, if it took 3 steps. But a red 3 which is 3 units from the track, a red 2 which is 2 units from the track, and a red 1 which is 1 unit from the track would land on the track itself; and the aim is quickly to find these points. The task is difficult, as the many black figures divert the attention, and as the red figures too near or too far are easily confused with those which are just at the dangerous distance.

As soon as this principle for the experiment was recognized as satisfactory, it was necessary to find a technical device by which a movement over this artificial track could be produced in such a way that the rapidity could be controlled by the subject of the experiment and at the same time measured. Again we had to try various forms of apparatus. Finally we found the following form most satisfactory. Twelve such cards, each provided with a handle, lie one above another under a glass plate through which the upper card can be seen. If this highest card is withdrawn, the second is exposed, and from below springs press the remaining cards against the glass plate. The glass plate with the 12 cards below lies in a black wooden box and is completely covered by a belt 8 inches broad made of heavy black velvet. This velvet belt moves over two cylinders at the front and the rear ends of the apparatus. In the centre of the belt is a window $4\frac{1}{2}$ inches wide and $2\frac{1}{2}$ inches high. If the front cylinder is turned by a metal crank, the velvet belt passes over the glass plate and the little window opening moves over the card with its track and figures. The whole breadth of the card, with its central track and its 4 units on either side, is visible through it over an area of 5 units in the length direction. If the man to be experimented on turns the crank with his right hand, the window slips over the whole length of the card, one part of the card after another becomes visible, and then he simply has to call the letters of those units in the track at which the red figures on either side would land, if they took the number of steps indicated by the digit. At the moment the window has reached Z on the card, the experimenter withdraws that card and the next becomes visible, as a second window in the belt appears at the lower end when the first disappears at the upper end. In this way the subject can turn his crank uninterruptedly until he has gone through the 12 cards. The experimenter notes down the numbers of the cards and the letters which the subject calls. Besides this, the number of seconds required for the whole experiment, from the beginning of the first card to the end of the twelfth, is measured with a stopwatch. This time is, of course, dependent upon the rapidity with which the crank is turned. The result of the experiment is accordingly expressed by three figures, the number of seconds, the number of omissions, that is, of places at which red figures would land on the track which were not noticed by the subject; and, thirdly, the number of incorrect places where letters were called in spite of the fact that no danger existed. In using the results, we may disregard this third figure and give our attention to the speed and the number of omissions.

The necessary condition for carrying out the experiments with this apparatus is a careful, quiet, practical explanation of the device. The experiment must not under any circumstances be started until the subject completely understands what he has to do and for what he has to look out. For this purpose I at first always show the man one card outside of the apparatus and explain to him the differences between the black and the red figures, and the counting of the steps, and show to him in a number of cases how some red figures do not reach the track, how others go beyond the track, and how some just land in danger on the track. As soon as he has completely understood the principle, we turn to the apparatus and he moves the window slowly over a test card and tries to find the dangerous spots, and I turn his attention to every case in which he has omitted one or has given an incorrect letter. We repeat this slowly until he completely masters the rules of the game. Only then is he allowed to start the experiment. I have never found a man with whom this preparation takes more than a few minutes.

THE BEST POSSIBLE MAN

After developing this method in the psycho-logical laboratory, I turned to the study of men actually in the service of a great electric railway company which supported my endeavors in the most cordial spirit. In accordance with my request, the company furnished me with a number of the best motormen in its service, men who for twenty years and more had performed their duties practically without accidents, and, on the other hand, with a large number of motormen who had only just escaped dismissal and whose record was characterized by many more or less important collisions or other accidents. Finally, we had men whose activity as motormen was neither especially good nor especially bad.

The test of the method lies first in the fact that the tried motormen agreed that they really pass through the experiment with the feeling which they have on their car. The necessity of looking out in both directions, right and left, for possible obstacles, of distinguishing those which move toward the track from the many which move along the track, the quick discrimination among the various rates of rapidity, the steady forward movement of the observation point, the constant temptation to give attention to those which are still too far away or to those which are so near that they will cross the track before the approach

74

of the car, in short, the whole complex situation with its demands on attention, imagination, and quick adjustment, soon brings them into an attitude which they themselves feel as identical with that in practical life. On the other hand, the results show a far-reaching correspondence between efficiency in the experiment and efficiency in the actual service. With a relatively small number of experiments this correspondence cannot be expected to be complete, the more as a large number of secondary features must enter which interfere with an exact correlation between experiment and standing in the railway company. We must consider, for instance, that those men whom the company naturally selects as models are men who have had twenty to thirty years of service without accidents, but consequently they are rather old men, who no longer have the elasticity of youth and are naturally less able to think themselves into an artificial situation like that of such an experiment, and who have been for a long time removed from contact with book work. It is therefore not surprising, but only to be expected, that such older, model men, while doing fair work in the test, are yet not seldom far surpassed by bright, quick, young motormen who are twenty years younger, even though they are not yet ideal motormen. Moreover, the standing in the company often depends upon features which have nothing to do with the mental make-up of the man, while the experiment has to be confined to those mental conditions which favor accidents. It is quite possible that a man may happen to experience a slight collision, even though no conditions for the accident were lying in his mental make-up. But we may go still further. The experiment refers to those sides of his mind which make him able to foresee the danger points, and that is decidedly the most essential factor and the one from which most can be hoped for the safety of the public. But this does not exclude the possibility that some other mental traits may become causes of accidents. The man may be too daring and may like to run risks, or he may still need discipline, or he may not be sufficiently acquainted with the local conditions. Any such secondary factors may cause some slight accidents with the man who shows rather fair results in the experimental test of his foresight. Finally, we must not forget that some men enter into such tests under a certain nervous tension and therefore may not show so well at the very first test as their mental equipment should allow. Hence it is decidedly desirable not to rely on the first test, but to repeat it. If those various interferences are taken into account, the correspondence between efficiency and the results of the tests is fairly satisfactory. It justified me in proposing that the experiments be continued and in regarding it as quite possible that later tests on the basis of this principle may be introduced at the employment of motormen.

A difficulty is presented by the valuation of the numerical results. The mere number of omissions alone cannot be decisive, as it is clear that no intelligent man would make any omissions if he should give an unlimited amount of time to it; for instance, if he were to spend fifteen minutes on those 12 cards. But this is the same thing as to say that a motorman would not run over any one if he were to drive his car one mile in an hour. The practical problem is to combine the greatest possible speed with the smallest number of oversights, and both factors must therefore be considered. The subject who makes relatively many mistakes but uses a very short time must be acknowledged to be as good as the man who makes fewer mistakes but takes a longer time. In the results which I have gathered in experiments with motormen, no one has gone through those 12 cards in a shorter time than 140 seconds, while the longest time was 427 seconds. On the other hand, no one of the motormen made less than 4 omissions, while the worst ones made 28 omissions. I abstract from one extreme case with 36 omissions. On the whole, we may say that the time fluctuates between 180 and 420, the mistakes between 4 and 28. The aim is to find a formula which gives full value to both factors and makes the material directly comparable in the form of one numerical value instead of the two. If we were simply to add the number of seconds and the number of omissions, the omissions would count far too little, inasmuch as 10 additional omissions would then mean no more than 10 additional seconds. On the other hand, if we were to multiply the two figures the omissions would mean by far too much, as the transition from 4 mistakes to 8 mistakes would then be as great a change as the transition from 200 to 400 seconds, that is, from the one extreme of time to the other. Evidently we balance both factors if we multiply the number of omissions by 10 and add them to the number of seconds. The variations between 4 and 28 omissions are 24 steps, which multiplied by 10 correspond to the 240 steps which lie between 180 and 420 seconds. On that basis any additional 50 seconds would be equal to 5 additional omissions. If of two men one takes 100 seconds less than his neighbor, he is equal to him in his ability to satisfy the demands of the service, if he makes 10 mistakes more.

On the basis of this calculation I find that the old, well-trained motormen come to a result of about 450, and I should consider that an average standard. This would mean that a man who uses 400 seconds would not be allowed to make more than 5 omissions, in 350 seconds not more than 10, in 300 not more than 15, in 250 not more than 20, under the condition that these are the results of the first set of experiments. Where there are more than 20 omissions made, mere quickness ought not to be allowed as a substitute. The man who takes 150 seconds and makes 30 mistakes would come up to the same standard level of 450. Yet his characteristics would probably not serve the interests of the service. He would speed up his car and would make better time than any one else, but would be liable to accidents. I should consider 20 mistakes with a time not longer than 250 as the permissible maximum. Among the younger motormen whom I examined, the best result was 290, in which 270 seconds were used and only 2 omissions made. Results below 350 may be considered as very good. One man, for instance, carried out the experiment in 237 seconds with 11 mistakes, which gives the result 347. From 350 to 450 may be counted as fair, 450 to 550 as mediocre, and over 550 as very poor. In the case of old men, who may be expected to adjust themselves less easily to artificial experiments, the limits may be shifted. If the experiments are made repeatedly, the valuation of the results must be changed accordingly. The training of the men in literary and mathematical work or in experimentation may be considered, as our experiments have shown that highly educated young people with long training in experimental observations can pass through the test much more quickly than any one of the motormen could. Among the most advanced graduate students who do research work in my Harvard laboratory there was no one whose result was more than 275, while, as I said, among all the motormen there was no one whose result was less than 290. The best result reached was by a student who passed through the test in 223 seconds with only 1 mistake, the total therefore being 233. Next came a student who did it in 215 seconds with 3 mistakes, total, 245; then in 228 seconds with 2 omissions, total, 248, and so on.

I recapitulate: With men on the educational level and at the age that comes in question for their first appointment in the service of an electric railway company, the test proposed ought to be applied according to this scheme. If they make more than 20 mistakes, they ought to be excluded; if they make less then 20 mistakes, the number of omissions is to be multiplied by 10 and added to the number of seconds. If the sum is less than 350, their mental fitness for the avoidance of accidents is very high, between 350 and 450 fair, and more than 550 not acceptable under any conditions. I submit this, however, with the emphasis on my previous statement that the investigation is still in its first stage, and that it will need a long coöperation between science and industry in order to determine the desirable modifications and special conditions which may become necessary in making the employment of men partly dependent upon such psychological tests. There can be no doubt that the experiments could be improved in many directions. But even in this first, not adequately tested, form, an experimental investigation of this kind which demands from each individual hardly 10 minutes would be sufficient to exclude perhaps one fourth of those who are nowadays accepted into the service as motormen. This 25 per cent of the applicants do not deserve any blame. In many other occupations they might render excellent service; they are neither careless nor reckless, and they do not act against instructions, but their psychical mechanism makes them unfit for that particular combination of attention and imagination which ought to be demanded for the special task of the motorman. If the many thousands of injury and the many hundreds of death cases could be reduced by such a test at least to a half, then the conditions of transportation would have been improved more than by any alterations in the technical apparatus, which usually are the only objects of interest in the discussion of specialists. The whole world of industry will have to learn the great lesson, that of the three great factors, material, machine, and man, the man is not the least, but the most important.

IX

EXPERIMENTS IN THE INTEREST OF SHIP SERVICE

WHERE the avoidance of accidents is in question, the test of a special experimental method can seldom be made dependent upon a comparison with practical results, as we do not want to wait until the candidate has brought human life into danger. The ordinary way of reaching the goal must therefore be an indirect one in such cases. For the study of motormen the conditions are exceptionally favorable, as hundreds of thousands of accidents occur every year, but another practical example may be chosen from a field where it is, indeed, impossible to correlate the results with actual misfortunes, because the dangerous situations occur seldom; and nevertheless on account of their importance they demand most serious study. I refer to the ship service, where the officer on the bridge may bring thousands into danger by one single slip of his mind. I turn to this as a further concrete illustration in order to characterize at once the lengths to which such vocational studies may advance.

One of the largest ship companies had approached me — long before the disaster of the Titanic occurred — with the question whether it would not be possible to find psychological methods for the elimination of such ship officers as would not be able to face an unexpected suddenly occurring complication. The director of the company wrote to me that in his experience the real danger for the great ships lies in the mental dispositions of the officers. They all know exactly what is to be done in every situation, but there are too many who do not react in the appropriate way when an unexpected combination of factors suddenly confronts them, such as the quick approach of a ship in the fog. He claimed that two different types ought to be excluded. There are ship officers who know the requirements excellently, but who are almost paralyzed when the dangerous conditions suddenly threaten. Their ability for action is inhibited. In one moment they want to act under the stimulus of one impression, but before the impulse is realized, some other perhaps rather indifferent impression forces itself on their minds and suggests the counteraction, and in this way they vacillate and remain inactive until it is too late to give the right order or to press the right button. The other type feels only the necessity for rapid action, and under the pressure of greatest haste, without clear thought, they jump to the first decision which rushes to their minds. Without carefully considering the conditions really given, they explode in an action which they would never have chosen in a state of quiet deliberation. They react on any accidental circumstance, just as at a fire men sometimes carry out and save the most useless parts of their belongings. Of course, beside these two types, there is the third type, the desirable one, the men who in the unexpected situation quickly review the totality of the factors in their relative importance and with almost instinctive certainty immediately come to the same decision to which they would have arrived after quiet thought. The director of the company insisted that it would be of highest importance for the ship service to discriminate these three types of human beings, and to make sure that there stand on the bridge of the ship only men who do not belong to those two dangerous classes. He turned to me with this request, as he had heard of the work toward economic psychology in the Harvard laboratory.

As the problem interested me, I carried on a long series of experiments in order to construct artificial conditions under which the mental process of decision in a complicated situation, especially the rapidity, correctness, and constancy of the decision, could be made measurable. I started from the conviction that this complex act of decision must stand in definite relation to a number of simpler mental functions. If, for instance, it stood in a clear definite relation to the process of association, or discrimination, or suggestibility, or perception, or memory, and so on, it would be rather easy to foresee the behavior of the individual in the act of decision, as every one of those other simple mental functions could be tested by routine methods of the psychological laboratory. This consideration led me to propose ramified investigations concerning the psychology of decision in its relation to the elementary mental processes. These studies by students of the laboratory are not yet completed. But I soon saw that they would be unfit for the solution of my practical problem, as we recognized that these relations between the complex act of decision and the elementary functions of the individual seem to have different form with different types of men.[12] If I was to approach the solution of the practical problem, accordingly, I had to reproduce in an experimental form the act of decision under complex conditions.

It seemed necessary to create a situation in which a number of quantitatively measurable factors were combined without any one of them forcing itself to consciousness as the most important.

The subject to be experimented on then has to decide as quickly as possible which of the factors is the relatively strongest one. As usual, here, too, I began with rather complicated material and only slowly did I simplify the apparatus until it finally took an entirely inconspicuous form. But this is surely the most desirable outcome for testing methods which are to be applied to large numbers of persons. Complicated instruments, for the handling of which special training is needed, are never so useful for practical purposes as the simple schemes which can be easily applied. The form of which I finally made use is the following. I work with 24 cards of the size of playing-cards. On the upper half of every one of these cards we have 4 rows of 12 capital letters, namely, A, E, O, and U in irregular repetition. On 4 cards, one of these vowels appears 21 times and each of the three others 9 times; on 8 cards, one appears 18 times and every one of the three others 10 times; on 8 cards, one appears 15 times and each of the others 11 times; and finally, on 4 cards one vowel appears 16 times, each of the three others 8 times, and besides them 8 different consonants are mixed in. The person to be tested has to distribute these 24 cards as quickly as possible in 4 piles, in such a way that in the first pile are placed all cards in which the letter A is most frequent, in the second those in which the letter E predominates, and so on. As a matter of course the result must never be secured by counting the letters. Any attempt to act against this prescription and secretly to begin counting would moreover delay the decision so long that the final result would be an unsatisfactory achievement anyhow. It would accordingly bring no advantage to the candidate.

We measure with a stopwatch in fifths of a second the time for the whole process from the subject's looking at the first card to his laying down of the last card, and, secondly, we record the number and the character of his mistakes, if cards are put into wrong piles. I have made the experiment with very many persons, and results show that those various mental traits which have been observed in the practical ship service come clearly to light under the conditions of this experiment. Some of the persons lose their heads entirely, and for many of them it is a painful activity for which they require a long time. Even if the number of mistakes is not considerable, they themselves have the feeling that they are not coming to a satisfactory decision, because their attention is pulled hither and thither so that they feel an inner mental paralysis. Some chance letters stand out and appear to them to be predominant, but in the next moment the attention is captured by some other letters which bring the suggestion that they are in the majority and that they present the most important factor. The outcome is that inner state of indecision which can become so fatal in practical life. Other subjects distribute the cards in piles at a relatively high speed, and they do it with the subjective feeling that they have indeed recognized at the first glance the predominant group of letters. The exact measurement of the results, however, shows that they commit many errors which would have been improbable after quiet consideration. Any small group of letters which catches their eye makes on them, under the pressure of their haste, such a strong impression that all the other letters are inhibited for the moment and the wrong decision is quickly made. Finally, we find a group of persons who carry out the experiment rather quickly and at the same time with few mistakes. It is characteristic of them to pass through it with the feeling that it is an agreeable and stimulating mental activity. In all cases the subjects feel themselves under the unified impression which results from all those 48 letters of the card together; and this is the reason why the qualitative manifoldness of a practical life situation can be compared with these intermingled, quantitatively determined groups of letters.

THE BEST POSSIBLE MAN

If I consider the general results of these experiments only with reference to the time-measurement, I should say that a person who completes the distribution of the cards in less than 80 seconds is quick in his decisions; from 80 to 150, moderately quick; from 150 to 250, slow and deliberate and rather too deliberate for situations which demand quick action; over 250 seconds, he would belong among those wavering persons who hesitate too long in a life situation which demands decision. The time which is needed for the mere distribution of the cards themselves plays a very small rôle compared with the time of the whole process, and can be neglected. In order to determine this, I asked all the subjects before they made the real experiment to distribute 24 other cards in 4 piles, on each of which one of the four letters, A, E, O, and U was printed only once. Hence no comparison of various factors was involved in this form of distribution. The average time for this ordinary sorting was about 20 seconds. Only rather quick individuals carried it out in less than 18 and only very slow ones needed more than 25 seconds. This maximum variation of 10 seconds is evidently insignificant, as the variations in the experiment amount to more than 200 seconds. But it is very characteristic that the results of the two experiments do not move parallel. Some persons, who are able to sort the cards on which only one of the 4 letters is printed very quickly, are rather slow when they sort the cards with the 48 letters for which the essential factor is the act of comparison. In the first case the training in card-playing also seems to have a certain influence, but in the second case, our real experiment on decision, this influence does not seem to exist.

We have emphasized from the start that it is no less important to give consideration to the number of mistakes. A mere rapidity of distribution with many mistakes characterizes, as we saw, a mental system which is just as unfit for practical purposes as one which acts with too great slowness. But it would not have been sufficient simply to ask how many cards were put into wrong piles. The special arrangement of the cards with four different types of combinations was introduced for the purpose of discriminating among mistakes of unequal seriousness. When one letter appeared 21 times and the three others only 9 times, it was surely much easier to make the decision than when the predominant letter appeared only 15 times and the other three each 11 times. The easier the right decision, the graver the mistake. Of course the valuation of these mistakes must be rather arbitrary. We decided to value as 4 every mistake in these cards on which the predominant

91

letter appears 21 times; as 3, a mistake in the 18 letter cards; as 2, a mistake in the 16 letter cards; and as 1, a mistake in the most difficult ones, the 15 letter cards. If the mistakes are calculated on this basis and are added together, a sum below 5 may indicate a very safe and perfectly reliable ability for decision; 5 to 12, satisfactory; 12 to 20, uncertain; and over 20, very poor. In order to take account of both factors, time and mistakes, we multiply the sum of the calculated mistakes by the number of seconds. If the product of these two figures is less than 400, it may be taken as a sign of perfect reliability in making very quick, correct decisions, in complex life situations; 400 to 1000 indicates the limits between which the ability for such decisions may be considered as normal and very satisfactory; 1000 to 2000, not good but still adequate; 2000 to 3000, unreliable, and over 3000, practically absent. It is clear that the real proof of the value of this method cannot be offered. This is just the reason why we selected this illustration as an example of the particular difficulty. Wrong decisions, that is, cases in which the man on the bridge waits too long before he makes his decision and thus causes a collision of ships by his delay, or in which he rushes blindly to a decision which he himself would have condemned after quiet deliberation, are rare. It would be impossible to group such men together for the purpose of the experiment and to compare their results with those of model captains, the more as experience has shown that an officer may have a stainless record for many years and yet may finally make a wrong decision which shows his faulty disposition. The test of the method must therefore be a somewhat indirect one. My aim was to compare the results of the experiments with the experiences of the various individuals which they themselves reported concerning their decisions in unexpected complicated situations, and moreover with the judgments of their friends whom I asked to describe what they would expect from the subjects under such conditions. The personal differences in these respects are extremely great, and are also evident in the midst of small groups of persons who may have great similarity in their education and training and in many other aspects of their lives.

Among the most advanced students of my research laboratory, for instance, all of whom have rather similar schooling and practically the same training in experimental work, the product of mistakes and seconds varied between 348 and 13,335. That smallest value occurred in a case in which the time was 116 seconds and the sum of the mistakes only 3, inasmuch as 3 cards of the most dif-

ficult group where the predominating letter occurred only 15 times were put in the wrong piles.
The shortest time among my laboratory students
was 58 seconds, but with this individual the sum
of the mistakes, calculated on the basis of the valuation agreed upon, was 13. The largest figure
mentioned resulted in a case in which the student
needed 381 seconds and yet made mistakes the
sum of which amounted to 35. It is characteristic
that the person with the smallest product felt a
distinct joy in the experiment, while the one with
the largest passed through painful minutes which
put him to real organic discomfort. If we arrange
the men simply in the order of these products, of
course we cannot recognize the various groups, as
those who are quick but make mistakes and those
who make few mistakes but act slowly may be represented by the same products. The coincidence
of the results with the self-characterization is frequently quite surprising. Every one has at some
time come into unexpected, suddenly arising situations and many have received in such moments
a very vivid impression of their own mental reaction. They know quite well that they could not
come to a decision quickly enough, or that they
rushed hastily to a wrong decision, or that in just
such instants a feeling of repose and security
came over them and that with sure instinct they

turned in the direction which they would have chosen after mature thought. The results of the experiments in sorting the cards confirmed this self-observation in such frequent cases that it may indeed be hoped that a more extended test of this method will prove its practical usefulness. It is clear that the field is a wide one, as these different types of mental dispositions must be of consequence not only in the ship service, but also to a certain degree in the railroad service and in many other industrial tasks.

We have emphasized from the start that as a matter of course such a tested function, while it is taken in its complex unity, is nevertheless not the only psychophysical disposition of significance. This is as true for the ship officer as it was for the motorman of the electric car. If we were to study all the mental dispositions necessary or desirable for the ship officer, we should find many other qualities which are accessible to the psychological investigation. The captain of the ship, for instance, is expected to recognize the direction of a vessel passing in the fog by the signals of the foghorn. But so far no one has given any attention to the psychological conditions of localization of sound, which were for a long while a much-studied problem of our psychological laboratories. We know how this localization is dependent upon the comparison of the two ears and what particular mistakes occur from the different sensibility of the two ears. Yet there are to-day men on the bridges of the ships who hear much better with one ear than with the other, but who still naïvely believe that, as they hear everything very distinctly with one ear, this normal ear is also sufficient for recognizing the direction of the sound. It is the same mistake which we frequently see among laborers whose vision has become defective in one of their eyes, or one of whose eyes is temporarily bandaged. They are convinced that the one good eye is sufficient for their industrial task, because they are able to recognize everything clearly and distinctly. They do not know that both the eyes together are necessary in order to produce that psychological combination by which the visual impression is projected into the right distance, and that in the factory they are always in danger of underestimating the distance of a wheel or some other part of the machine and of letting the hand slip between the wheels or knives. The results of experimental psychology will have to be introduced systematically into the study of the fitness of the personality from the lowest to the highest technical activity and from the simplest sensory function to the most complex mental achievement.

X

EXPERIMENTS IN THE INTEREST OF
TELEPHONE SERVICE

OUR plan was to illustrate the possibility of applying psychological experiments to the selection of fit applicants also in cases in which not one characteristic mental function stands out, but in which a large number of relatively independent mental activities are in play. I choose as an illustration of such cases the work of the employees at the telephone switchboard. A study of the psychological factors in this work is strongly suggested by the practical interests of the telephone companies, and may be looked on here exclusively from this point of view. The user of the telephone is little inclined to consider how many actions have to be carried out in the central office before the connection is made and finally broken again. From the moment when the speaker takes off the receiver to the cutting off of the connection, fourteen separate psychophysical processes are necessary in the typical case, and even then it is presupposed that the telephone girl understood the exchange and number correctly. It is a common experience of the companies that these demands cannot be satisfactorily fulfilled when a telephone girl has to handle more than 225 calls in an hour. The official statistics show that this figure is exceeded in not infrequent cases,[13] in extreme cases the number may even rise beyond 300. Moreover, in short periods of reinforced demands it may happen that for a few minutes even the rapidity of 10 calls in a minute is reached. Normally the burden is divided among the employees in such a way that about 150 calls fall to each one in an hour, and that this figure is passed considerably only in one morning and one evening hour. A skillful distribution of pauses and ample arrangements for rest, usually together with very excellent hygienic conditions, make it possible for the fit persons to be able to carry on this work without over-fatigue from 8 to 9 hours a day. On the other hand, it is only natural that such rapid and yet subtle activity under such high tension, where especially the quick localization of the correct hole is a difficult and yet indispensable part, can be carried out only by a relatively small number of human nervous systems. The inability to keep attention at such a high point for a long while, or to perform such rapid movements, or to retain the numbers correctly, does not lead to fatal accidents like those in the case of the unfit motormen, but it does lead to fatigue and finally to a nervous breakdown of the employees and to confusion in the service. The result is that the company is continually obliged to dismiss a considerable proportion of those who have entered the service and who have spent some months in going through the training school of the company. As one single company, the Bell Telephone Company, employs 16,000 operators, the problem is an expansive one, and it has bearing on the health of the employees as well as on the patience of the subscribers. But above all it refers to the economic interests of the company, inasmuch as every girl who satisfies the entrance conditions of hearing and sight, of school education and general personal appearance, receives some salary throughout the months of training in the telephone school. Since during the first half-year, in which the employee still works entirely under supervision, more than a third of those who had originally entered leave, partly on account of unfitness and inability, partly on account of overfatigue or similar reasons, the economic disadvantage to the company is evidently a very great one. The candidates are paid for months of mere training, and they themselves waste their energy and time with practice in a kind of labor which cannot be serviceable to them in any other economic activity. Under these circumstances it is not surprising that one city system approached me with the question whether it would not interest me from a scientific point of view to examine how far the mental fitness of the employees could be determined beforehand through experimental means.

After carefully observing the service in the central office for a while, I came to the conviction that it would not be appropriate here to reproduce the activity at the switchboard in the experiment, but that it would be more desirable to resolve that whole function into its elements and to undertake the experimental test of a whole series of elementary mental dispositions. Every one of these mental acts can then be examined according to well-known laboratory methods without giving to the experiments any direct relation to the characteristic telephone operation as such. I carried on the first series of experiments with about thirty young women who a short time before had entered into the telephone training school, where they are admitted only at the age between seventeen and twenty-three years. I examined them with reference to eight different psychophysical functions. In saying this, I abstract from all those measurements and tests which had somewhat anthropometric character, such as the measurement of the length of the fingers, the rapidity of breathing, the rapidity of pulse, the acuity of vision and of hearing, the distinctness of the pronunciation, and so on. A part of the psychological tests were carried on in individual examinations, but the greater part with the whole class together.

These common tests referred to memory, attention, intelligence, exactitude, and rapidity. I may characterize the experiments in a few words. The memory examination consisted of reading to the whole class at first two numbers of 4 digits, then two of 5 digits, then two of 6 digits, and so on up to figures of 12 digits, and demanding that they be written down as soon as a signal was given. The experiments on attention, which in this case of the telephone operators seemed to me especially significant, made use of a method the principle of which has frequently been applied in the experimental psychology of individual differences and which I adjusted to our special needs. The requirement is to cross out a particular letter in a connected text. Every one of the thirty women in the classroom received the same first page of a newspaper of that morning. I emphasize that it was a new paper, as the newness of the content was to secure the desired distraction of the attention. As soon as the signal was given, each one of the girls had to cross out with a pencil every "a" in the text for six minutes. After a certain time, a bell signal was given and each then had to begin a new column. In this way we could find out, first, how many letters were correctly crossed out in those six minutes, secondly, how many letters were overlooked, and, thirdly, how the recognition and the oversight were distributed in the various parts of the text. In every one of these three directions strong individual differences were indeed noticeable. Some persons crossed out many, but also overlooked many, others overlooked hardly any of the "a's," but proceeded very slowly so that the total number of the crossed-out letters was small. Moreover, it was found that some at first do poor work, but soon reach a point at which their attention remains on a high level; others begin with a relatively high achievement, but after a short time their attention flags, and the number of crossed-out letters becomes smaller or the number of unnoticed, overlooked letters increases. Fluctuations of attention, deficiencies, and strong points can be discovered in much detail.

The third test which was tried with the whole class referred to the intelligence of the individuals. Discussion of the question how to test intelligence in general would quickly lead us into as yet unsettled controversies. It is a chapter of the psychology of tests which, especially in the service of pedagogy but to a certain degree also in the service of medicine, has been more carefully elaborated than any other. Often it has been contested whether we have any right to speak of one general central intelligence factor, and whether this apparently unified activity ought not to be resolved into a series of mere elementary processes. The newer pedagogical investigations, however, speak in favor of the view that besides all special processes, or rather, above all of them, an ability must be recognized which cannot be divided any further, and by which the individual adjusts his knowledge, his experiences, and his dispositions to the changing purposes of life. The grading of the pupils in a class usually expresses this differentiation of the intelligence; and while the differences of industry or of mere memory and similar secondary features may sometimes interfere, it remains after all not difficult for an observant teacher to grade the pupils of his class, whom he knows well, according to their general intelligence. The psychological experiments carried on in the schoolroom have demonstrated that this ability can be tested by the measurement of some very simple mental activities. The best method would be the one which would allow the experimenter, on the basis of a single experiment, to grade the individuals in the same order in which they appear in the record of the teacher. Among the various proposed schemes for this purpose the figures suggest that the most reliable one is the following method, the results of which show the highest agreement between the rank order based on the experiments and the rank order of the teachers.[14] The experiment consists in reading to the pupils a long series of pairs of words of which the two members of the pair always logically belong together. Later, one word of each pair will be read to them and they have to write down the word which belonged with it in the pair. This is not a simple experiment on memory. The tests have shown that if instead of logically connected words simply disconnected chance words are offered and reproduced, no one can keep such a long series of pairs in mind, while with the words which have related meaning, the most intelligent pupils can master the whole series. The very favorable results which this method had yielded in the classroom made me decide to try it in this case too. I chose for an experiment 24 pairs of words from the sphere of experience of the girls to be tested. Two further class experiments belonged rather to the periphery of psychology. The exactitude of space-perception was measured by demanding that each divide first the long and then the short edge of a folio sheet into two equal halves by a pencil mark. And finally, to measure the rapidity of movement, it was demanded that every one make with a pencil on the paper zigzag movements of a particular size during the ten seconds from one signal to another.

After these class experiments I turned to individual tests. First, every girl had to sort a pack of 48 cards into 4 piles as quickly as possible. The time was measured in fifths of a second. The following experiment which referred to the accuracy of movement impulses demanded that every one try to reach with the point of a pencil 3 different points on the table in the rhythm of metronome beats. On each of these three places a sheet of paper was fixed with a fine cross in the middle. The pencil should hit the crossing point, and the marks on the paper indicated how far the movement had fallen short of the goal. One of these movements demanded the full extension of the arm and the other two had to be made with half-bent arm. I introduced this last test because the hitting of the right holes in the switchboard of the telephone office is of great importance. The last individual experiment was an association test. I called six words like "book," "house," "rain," and had them speak the first word which came to their minds. The time was measured in fifths of a second only, as subtler experiments, for which hundredths of a second would have to be considered, were not needed.

In studying the results so far as the memory experiments were concerned, we found that it would be useless to consider the figures with more than 10 digits. We took the results only of those with 8, 9, and 10 digits. There were 54 possibilities of mistakes. The smallest number of actual mistakes was 2, the largest, 29. In the experiment on attention made with the crossing-out of letters, we found that the smallest number of correctly marked letters was 107, the largest number in the six minutes, 272; the smallest number of overlooked letters was 2, the largest, 135; but this last case of abnormal carelessness stood quite isolated. On the whole, the number of overlooked letters fluctuated between 5 and 60. If both results, those of the crossed-out and those of the overlooked letters, are brought into relation, we find that the best results were a case of 236 letters marked, with only 2 overlooked, and one of 257 marked, with 4 overlooked. The very interesting details as to the various types of attention which we see in the distribution of mistakes over the six minutes were not taken into our final table. The word experiments by which we tested the intelligence showed that no one was able to reproduce more than 22 of the 24 words. The smallest num-

ber of words remembered was 7. The mistakes
in the perception of distances fluctuated between
1 and 14 millimeters; the time for the sorting of
the 48 cards, between 35 and 58 seconds; the association-time for the 6 associated words taken
together was between 9 and 21 seconds. The
pointing experiments could not be made use of in
this first series, as it was found that quite a number of participants were unable to perform the act
with the rapidity demanded.

Several ways were open to make mathematical
use of these results. I preferred the simplest way.
I calculated the grade of the girls for each of these
achievements. The same candidate who stood in
the 7th place in the memory experiment was in the
15th place with reference to the number of letters
marked, in the 3rd place with reference to the letters overlooked, in the 21st place with reference to
the number of word pairs which she had grasped,
in the 11th place with reference to the exactitude
of space-perception, in the 16th place with reference to the association-time, and in the 6th place
with reference to the time of sorting. As soon as
we had all these independent grades,we calculated
the average and in this way ultimately gained a
common order of grading. It is evident that this
kind of calculation contains accidental factors,
especially as a consequence of the fact that we

give equal value to every one of these results. It might be better, for instance, to attribute a higher value to the attention experiment or to the intelligence experiment. This could be done by multiplying the results of some of these grades by 2 or by 3, which would bring the high or low grade of a girl for a particular function to stronger influence in the final result. But in this first trial I contented myself with the simplest uniform scheme in order to exclude all arbitrariness, and therefore considered the mere average of all the grades as the expression of the experimental result.

With this average rank list, we compared the practical results of the telephone company after three months had passed. These three months had been sufficient to secure at least a certain discrimination between the best, the average, and the unfit. The result of this comparison was on the whole satisfactory. First, the skeptical telephone company had mixed with the class a number of women who had been in the service for a long while and had even been selected as teachers in the telephone school. I did not know, in figuring out the results, which of the participants in the experiments these particularly gifted outsiders were. If the psychological experiments had brought the result that these individuals who stood so high in the estimation of the telephone company ranked low in the laboratory experiment, it would have reflected strongly on the reliability of the laboratory method. The results showed, on the contrary, that these women who had proved most able in practical service stood at the top of our list. Correspondingly, those who stood the lowest in our psychological rank list had in the mean time been found unfit in practical service and had either left the company of their own accord or else had been eliminated. The agreement, to be sure, was not a perfect one. One of the list of women stood rather low in the psychological list, while the office reported that so far she had done fair work in the service, and two others to whom the psychological laboratory gave a good testimonial were considered by the telephone office as only fair.

But it is evident that certain disagreements would have occurred even with a more ideal method, as on the one side no final achievement in practical service can be given after only three months, and because on the other side a large number of secondary factors may enter which entirely overshadow the mere question of psychophysical fitness. Poor health, for instance, may hinder even the most fit individual from doing satisfactory work, and extreme industry and energetic will may for a while lead even the unfit to fair achievement, which, to be sure, is likely to be coupled with a dangerous exhaustion. The slight disagreements between the psychological results and the practical valuation, therefore, do not in the least speak against the significance of such a method. On the other hand, I emphasize that this first series meant only the beginning of the investigation, and it can hardly be expected that at such a first approach the best and most suitable methods would at once be hit upon. A continuation of the work will surely lead to much better combinations of test experiments and to better adjusted schemes. But it would be most desirable that such studies be undertaken at various places according to various schemes in order to come nearer to the solution of a problem which is economically important to the whole public and to many thousands of employees. As soon as methods are really perfected it would seem not at all impossible that by a short experiment of a few minutes thousands of applicants might be saved long months of study and training which are completely wasted. For us here the detailed analysis of this particular case did not mean a suggestion to use to-day in the telephone offices of the country the special scheme which we applied, but it stood only as a clear, simple illustration of a method by which not the specific work itself is tested, but by which the industrial work of the individual is resolved into a long series of parallel functions each one of which is tested independently. The experimental aid which the laboratory has to supply in such cases is not a newly invented device, such as we needed in the case of the motormen, but simply the methods well known as so-called mental tests.

The experiments with such tests by which single mental functions are measured approximately in short quick examinations, has been much discussed in psychological circles. For a long while the thorough scholars remained very reluctant to accept such an apparently superficial scheme, when these tests were proposed especially for the pedagogical interests of the schoolroom. It was a time in which the scientific efforts were completely devoted to the general problems of the human mind and in which individual differences were very little considered. Moreover, the questions of applied psychology still seemed so far distant that the true scholar instinctively took his standards from the methods of purely theoretical research. Seen from such a point of view, it could not be denied that the tests were not sufficient to give us a complete scientific analysis of the personality in its subtler structure. The theorists knew too well that if the reactions, or associations, or memories, or tendencies of attention, or emotions of a subject were measured really with that scientific thoroughness which is the ideal of research, long months of experiments would be needed, and little could be hoped for from tests to be performed in half an hour. But this somewhat haughty reserve which was quite justified twenty years ago has become obsolete and would be meaningless to-day. On the one side the methods themselves have been multiplied; for each mental act like memory, attention, and so on, dozens of well-studied tests are at our disposal, which are adjusted to the finest ramifications of the functions.[15] On the other side the interest in individual differences and in applied psychology has steadily grown, and through it an understanding for the real meaning of the tests has been gained. Their value, indeed, lies exclusively in their relation to the practical problems. Where theoretical questions are to be answered and scientific studies concerning the laws and variations of the mind are to be undertaken, the long series of laboratory experiments carried on with patience and devotion are indispensable and can never be replaced by the short-cut methods of the tests. But where practical tasks of pedagogy or jurisprudence or medicine, or especially of commerce and industry, are before us, the method of tests ought to be sovereign. It can be adapted to the special situations and can succeed perfectly, if the task is to discover the outlines of the mental individuality for particular practical work.

The only real difficulty of the method lies in the ease with which it can be used. A device which presupposes complicated instruments deters the layman and will be used only by those who are well trained. Moreover, the amateur would not think of constructing and adapting such apparatus himself. But when nothing is necessary but to use words or numbers or syllables or pictures, or, as in those experiments which we just described, newspapers and so on, any one feels justified in applying the scheme or in replacing it by a new apparently better one according to his caprice. The manifoldness of the proposed tests for special functions is therefore enormous to-day. What is needed now is surely much more that order be brought into this chaos of propositions, and that definite norms and standards be secured for certain chief examinations, than that the number of variations simply be increased.

The chief danger, moreover, lies in the fact that those who are not accustomed to psychological laboratory research are easily misled. They fancy that such an experiment can be carried out in a mere mechanical way without careful study of all the conditions and accompanying circumstances. Thereby a certain crudeness of procedure may enter which is not at all suggested by the test method itself. The psychological layman too seldom recognizes how many other psychical functions may play a rôle in the result of the experiment beside the one which is interesting him at that moment. The well-schooled laboratory worker almost automatically gives consideration to all such secondary circumstances. While his experiments may refer to the process of memory, he will yet at the same time carefully consider the particular situation as to the emotional setting of the subject, as to his attention, as to his preceding experience, as to his intelligence, as to his physiological condition, and many other factors which may have indirect influence even on the simplest memory test. Hence the real performance of the experiments ought to be undertaken only by those who are thoroughly familiar and well trained in psychological research. And they alone, moreover, can decide what particular form such an experiment ought to take in a given practical situation. It must be left to them, for instance, to judge in which cases the mental function of economic importance ought to be tested after being resolved into its components and in which it ought to be examined in its characteristic unity.

XI

WHILE the psychologists have to perform the actual labor, the representatives of practical life are much better able to indicate the points at which the psychological levers ought to be applied. In the past year I have sought contact with several hundred large concerns in America which belong to many different industrial realms. My time did not allow me personal observation in so many cases, but everywhere I begged for information from the leading men. I asked in individual letters for the particular psychological qualities which from the standpoint of the management seemed essential for the various kinds of labor in their establishments. I always inquired to what extent consideration was given to such psychological points of view at the appointment of applicants, and asked for material concerning the question how far individuals who proved to be unfit for one kind of labor showed fitness at other kinds of work. The replies which I received from all sides varied from a few meaningless lines to long documents, which in some cases were composed of detailed reports from all the department chiefs of a particular concern.

CONTRIBUTIONS FROM MEN OF AFFAIRS

The common fundamental turn was decidedly a feeling of strong interest in the formulation of the question, which was practically new to all of them. Whether the answer came from paper mills or machine shops, from meat-packing houses or from breweries, from electrical or chemical mills, from railroad or mining companies, from department stores or from publishing houses, everywhere it was acknowledged that they had given hardly any conscious attention to the real psychological dispositions of their employees. They had of course noticed whether their men were industrious or lazy, honest or dishonest, skillful or clumsy, peaceful or quarrelsome people, but I had emphasized from the start in all my letters that such points of view were not before my mind. The mental qualities for which I asked were the psychological functions of attention, memory, ideas, imagination, feeling, volition, suggestibility, ability to learn, ability to discriminate, judgment, space-sense, time-sense, and so on. It would lead too far here to discuss why these two groups of characteristics indeed belong to two different aspects of mental life, and why only the latter is strictly psychological. The way in which the management is accustomed to look on their men is the practical way of ordinary life, in which we try to understand our neighbor by entering into the meaning of his mental functions and by seeking to grasp what his aim is. But such an interpretation of the other man's mind is not a psychological analysis. It gives us the purposes of his inner life, but does not show us its structure and its component parts. We can abstract from interpreting and appreciating in order to describe the elements of the mind which in themselves have no meaning and no value, but which are the only important factors, if we are to determine psychologically what we may expect from the individual.

While the replies to my letters showed that hardly any attention had so far been given to such problems of objective psychology in the industrial concerns, it became evident that the managers felt distinctly that here a problem was touched which must be of highest importance for economic success. From many different sides willingness was shown to study the problem of employment under the psychological aspect. As my material came mostly from very large establishments in which labor of very many different kinds is carried on side by side, of course I frequently received the assurance that whenever an industrious energetic man is unsuccessful in one kind of work, a trial is made with him in another department, and that by such shifting the right place can often be found for him. Young people, to whom, in spite of long trial and the best will, it seems impossible to supply certain automatic machines, become excellent workers at much more difficult labor in the same establishment. Women who are apparently careless and inattentive when they have to distribute their attention over a number of operations do high-class work when they are engaged in a single activity; and in other cases the opposite is reported.

I may mention a few concrete chance illustrations. In a pencil factory the women in one department have to grasp with one movement a dozen pencils, no more and no less. Some learn this at once without effort, and they earn high wages; others never can learn it in spite of repeated trials. If those who fail in this department are transferred, for instance, to the department where the gold-leaf is most carefully to be applied to the pencils before stamping, very often they show great fitness in spite of the extreme exactitude needed for this work. To show how often activities which appear extremely similar may demand different individuals, if the work is based on different psychical functions, I may refer to a report from one of the largest establishments in the country. In the accounting department a large number of girls are occupied with looking over hundreds of thousands of slips from which the weekly pay-list is compiled. Each slip contains six figures and small groups of twenty slips have to be looked through to see whether those six figures on each correspond. With moistened forefinger they turn up the slips one by one in much the same manner that a bank clerk counts money. A good sorter will turn up the slips so rapidly that a bystander is unable to read a single figure, and yet she will not overlook an error in thousands of slips. After the slips are sorted, the operation of obtaining the totals on each order number is performed with the aid of an adding machine. The machine operator rolls up the slips of the pile with the thumb of her left hand and transfers the amount to the proper keys of the machine. It has been found that the most rapid and accurate girls at sorting are not seldom useless on the machines. They press the wrong keys and make errors in copying the total from the machine indicators to the file-card. On the other hand, some of the best machine operators are very slow and inaccurate at the sorting table. Girls have been found very poor at the work at which they were first set, and very successful and efficient as soon as they had been transferred from the one to the other.

Examples of this kind might be heaped up without end. But while the very large establishments demonstrate by such reports only that they can find somewhere a fit place for every able workingman if they take enough trouble to seek for it, after all the essential element of the reports remains, that successful achievement depends upon personal mental traits which cannot be acquired by mere good will and training. In view of this fact it is much more important that by far the majority of establishments have not such a great manifoldness of activities under one roof. The workingman who is a failure in the work which he undertook would usually have no opportunity to show his strong sides in the same factory, or at least to be protected against the consequences of his weak points. If his achievement is deficient in quality or quantity, he generally loses his place and makes a new trial in another factory under the same accidental conditions, without any deeper insight into his particular psychical traits and their relation to special industrial activities. But even in the large concerns, in which many kinds of labor are needed side by side, it is not the rule but a rare exception when the individual is systematically shifted to the psychologically correct place. A whole combination of conditions is necessary for that. If his mental unfitness makes him unsuccessful in one place, the position for which he is fit must happen to be vacant. Moreover, he himself must like that other kind of work, and above all the foreman must recognize his particular fitness. In a few model factories in which the apprentice system is developed in the spirit of advanced sociological ideas, for instance, in the Lynn factory of the General Electric Company, such systematic efforts are being carried on and show fair results. But the regulation plan seems to be a haphazard lack of plan, and even the best endeavors probably fall short of what may be attained by the introduction of scientific psychological methods. So far in most factories the laborer who is not doing well simply loses his position, and by such an unfortunate experience he is not mentally enriched but impoverished, as he has lost much of his self-confidence and of his joy in labor.

If this limitless waste of human material, this pitiable crushing of joy in the day's work, and this crippling of the economic output is at last to be reduced, indeed nothing is more needed than a careful scrutiny of the various psychophysical functions involved in the work. A mere classification of the industrial occupations according to the classes of manufactured objects would be of no value for this need, as often a small industrial concern may embrace occupations which are based on many different psychophysical functions. A harvester consists of two hundred and fifty different parts, and almost every one of these parts demands a long series of manufacturing processes. Thousands of different kinds of labor are thus combined in one factory and each process demands for the best work particular psychophysical traits, even though many of them can be carried out by quite unskilled laborers. In a large manufacturing establishment the manager assured me only recently that more than half a million different acts have to be performed in order to complete the goods of that factory. On the other hand, it evidently is proper to form larger groups in which processes are brought together which are similar with reference to the mental activity needed, while they may be dissimilar from the standpoint of industrial technique.

This analysis of the special processes can be furthered best by the coöperation of the experienced men of industry. Many of the replies which I received contained quite elaborated contributions to such a study of various industrial processes from a psychological point of view. They sometimes covered the ground from the simplest activity to the subtlest and most difficult economic tasks, and this, not only with reference to the functions of the laborer, but also even with reference to the function of the industrial manager. The outsider can see these psychological requirements of the particular occupation only in crude outlines. The subtler nuances of differences between tasks can be gained only by an intimate knowledge of the industry. Again I may give an illustration. In the case of a well-known type-setting machine, thousands of which are in daily use, I had the impression that the rapidity of the performance was dependent upon the quickness of the finger reaction. The managers, on the other hand, have found that the most essential condition for speed in the whole work is the ability to retain a large number of words in memory before they are set. The man who presses the keys rather slowly advances more rapidly than another who moves his fingers quickly, but must make many pauses in order to find his place in the manuscript and to provide himself with new words.

The factors which are to be brought into correlation are, accordingly, first, the actual experiences of the managers, secondly, the observations of skilled psychologists in the industrial concerns, thirdly, psychological and experimental investigations with successful and unsuccessful laborers, and, fourthly, experimental studies of the normal variability. If such a programme is to be realized in detail, it will be necessary to discriminate carefully between those mental traits of the personality which must be accredited to a lasting inherited disposition and such as have been developed under the influences of the surroundings, by education and training, by bad or good stimuli from the community. While those acquired traits may have become relatively lasting dispositions, their transformation is, after all, possible, and the limits in which changes may be expected will have to be found out by exact studies. Individual psychological rhythm, attention and emotion, memory and will energy, disposition to fatigue and to restoration, imagination, suggestibility and initiative, and many other features will have to be examined in their relation to the special economic aims.

Too much emphasis cannot be laid on another function as well, the experimental testing of which has only recently been started. I refer to the difference in the individual ability of men to profit from training. If we test an individual at a certain point in his life with regard to a variable ability, our result must be dependent upon three factors, the original disposition for the performance, the original disposition for the advance by training, and the training itself actually passed through up to that moment. A small amount of antecedent training for the particular task together with a

125

high ability to profit from repetition may be a better reason for the appointment of a man than a long training with small ability to profit from schooling, in spite of the fact that his actual achievement at this time may be in the first case smaller than in the second. He will do less at first, but he promises to outrank the other man after a period of further training. Special experiments must be carried on and have been actually started to determine this plasticity of the psychophysical apparatus as an independent inborn trait of the individual.[16]

This invasion of psychology into the field of economic activities is still so little advanced that the thought of a real distribution of the wage-earners among the various commercial and industrial positions on the basis of psychological tests would lead far beyond the present possibilities. Moreover, many factors would interfere with its being carried out consistently, even if a much higher stage of experimental research were reached. The thousands of social and local reasons which influence the choice of a vocation to-day would to a certain degree remain in force also in a period of better psychological analysis. Moreover, the personal inclinations and interests naturally would and ought to remain the mainspring of economic action. This inclination, which gives so much of the joy in labor, is by no means necessarily coincident with those psychophysical dispositions which insure the most successful work. Political economists have found this out repeatedly from their statistical inquiries. Very careful studies of the textile industry in Germany carried out in recent years [17] yielded the result that the intelligent, highly trained textile laborer often dislikes his work the more, the more he shows ability for it, this ability being measured by the wages the individuals earn at piecework. The wage and the emotional attitude were not seldom inversely related. Those who were able to produce by far more than others and accordingly earned the most were sometimes the very ones who hated the work, while the less skillful workers earned less but enjoyed the work more. The consulting economic psychologist will, therefore, at first reasonably confine himself to warning the misfits at an early time. Even within these limits his service can be useful to both parties, the employers and the employees. He will only slowly reach the stage at which this negative warning may be supplemented by positive suggestions, as to the commercial industrial activities for which the psychophysical dispositions promise particular success.

A real assumption of responsibility for success

of course cannot be risked by the psychologist, inasmuch as the man who may be fitted for a task by his mental working dispositions may nevertheless destroy his chances for success by secondary personal traits. He may be dishonest, or dissipated, or a drinker, or a fighter, or physically ill. Finally, we ought not to forget that all such efforts to adjust to one another the psychological traits and the requirements of the work can never have reference to the extreme variations of human traits. The exceptionally talented man knows anyhow where he belongs, and the exceptionally untalented one will be excluded anyhow. The psychological aid in the selection of the fit refers only to the remaining four fifths of mankind for whom the chances of success can indeed be increased as soon as the psychological personal equation is systematically and with scientific exactitude brought into the calculation of the life development. How far a part of this effort will have to be undertaken by the school is a social problem which must be considered from various points of view. Its discussion would lead us beyond the limits of our present inquiry, but it seems probable that the real psychological laboratory experiment in the service of vocational guidance does not belong in the schoolroom itself, but ought to be left to special municipal institutions.

XII

INDIVIDUALS AND GROUPS

ONE point here must not be overlooked. The effort to discover the personal structure of the individual in the interest of his vocational chance does not always necessarily involve a direct analysis of his individuality, as material of some value can be gained indirectly. Such indirect knowledge of a man's mental traits may be secured first of all through referring the man to the groups to which he belongs and inquiring into the characteristic traits of those groups. The psychology of human variations gives not only an account of the differences from person to person, but studies no less the psychical inequalities of the races, of the nations, of the ages, of the professions, and so on. If an economic activity demands a combination of mental traits, we may take it for granted that an individual will be fit for the work as soon as we find out that he belongs to a group in which these required mental traits habitually occur. Such a judgment based on group psychology can of course be no more than a mere approach to a solution of the problem, as the psychical qualities may vary strongly in the midst of the group. The special individual may happen to stand at the extreme limit of the group, and the traits which are usually characteristic of it may be very little developed or entirely lacking in his special case. We may know that the inhabitants of a special country are rather alert, and yet the particular individual with whom we have to deal may be clumsy and phlegmatic. The interests of economy will, therefore, be served by such considerations of group psychology only if the employment, not of a single person, but of a large number, is in question, as it is most probable that the average character will show itself in a sufficient degree as soon as many members of the group are involved.

Even in this case the presupposition ought to be that the average characteristics are found out with scientific exactitude by statistical and experimental methods, and not that they are simply deduced from superficial impressions. I have found that just this race psychological diagnosis is frequently made in factories with great superficiality. Some of the American industrial centres offer extremely favorable conditions for the comparative study of nationality. I have visited many manufacturing establishments in which almost all workers are immigrants from foreign countries and in which up to twenty different nationalities are represented. The employment officers there easily develop some psychological theories on the basis of which they are convinced that they are selecting the men with especial skill, knowing for each in which department he will be most successful. They consider it settled that for a particular kind of activity the Italians are the best, and for another, the Irish, and for a third, the Hungarians, and for a fourth, the Russian Jews. But as soon as these factory secrets have been revealed, you may be surprised to find that in the next factory a decidedly different classification of the wage-earners is in force. In a gigantic manufacturing concern, I received the definite information that the Swedish laborers are preferable wherever a steady eye is needed, and in another large factory on the same street I was assured that just the Swedes are unfit for such work. Sometimes this diversity of opinion is the result of different points of view. In one factory in which a certain industrial operation is rather dangerous, they told me that they took no southern Europeans, especially no Italians and Greeks, because they are too hasty and careless in their movements, while they gladly filled the places with Irishmen. In a quite similar factory, on the other hand, they had a prejudice against the Irishmen alone for this work, because the Irish laborers are too willing to run a risk and to expose themselves to danger. Probably both psychological observations are on the whole correct, but in the first factory only the one and in the second factory only the other was recognized. Much more thorough statistical inquiries than those which as yet exist, especially as to the actual differences of wages and piecework for wage-earners of various nationalities, would have to furnish a basis for such race psychological statements, until the time arrives when the psychological experiment comes to its own.

In a similar way so far we have to rely on general theories of group psychology when the psychological differences of the sexes are to be reckoned with in economic interests. So long as laboratory methods for individual tests are not usual, the mental analysis of the general groups of men and women must form the background for industrial decisions. To be sure, it is not difficult to emphasize certain mental traits as characteristic of women in general in contrast to men in general, and to relate them to certain fundamental tendencies of their psychophysical organism. As soon as this is done, it is easy theoretically to deduce that certain industrial functions are excellently adapted to the minds of women and that certain others stand in striking antagonism to them. If the employment of large numbers is in question, and average values alone are involved, such a decision on the basis of group psychology may be adequate. In most factories this vague sex psychology, to be sure, usually with a strong admixture of wage questions, suggests for which machines men and for which women ought to be employed. But here again it is not at all improbable that in the case of a particular woman the traditional group value may be entirely misleading and the personality accordingly unfit for the place. Only the subtle psychological individual analysis can overcome the superficial prejudices of group psychology. The situation lies differently when problems of economic policy are before us. Such general policies as, for instance, colonial politics, or immigration politics, or politics concerned with city and rural communities, or with coast and mountain population, will always have to be based on group psychology as far as the economic problems are involved, inasmuch as they refer to the average and not to the individual differences.

Finally, another indirect scheme to determine the personal qualities needed for economic efficiency may be suggested by the psychology of the typical correlations of human traits. We have seen that group psychology proclaims that a certain individual probably has certain traits because he belongs to this or that nation or to this or that otherwise well-known group. Correlation psychology proclaims that a particular individual possesses or does not possess certain traits because he shows or does not show some other definite qualities. A correlation, for instance, which the commercial world often presupposes, may exist between individual traits and the hand-writing. Graphologists are convinced that a certain loop or flourish, or the steepness or the length of the letters, or the position of the i dot, is a definite indication that the writer possesses certain qualities of personality; and if just these qualities are essential requirements for the position, the impression of the handwriting in a letter may be taken as a sufficient basis for appointment. The scientist has reason to look upon this particular case of graphological correlation with distrust. Yet even he may acknowledge that certain correlations exist between the neatness, carefulness, uniformity, energy, and similar features of the letter, and the general carefulness, steadiness, neatness, and energy of the personality.

However, the laboratory psychologists nowadays have gone far beyond such superficial claims for correlations of symptoms. With experimental and statistical methods they have gathered ample material which demonstrates the exact degree of probability with which we have a right to expect that certain qualities will occur together. Theoretically we may take it for granted that those traits which are always present together or absent together ultimately have a common mental root. Yet practically they appear as two independent traits, and therefore it remains important to know that, if we can find one of them, we may be sure that the other will exist there too. Inasmuch as the one of the two traits may be easily detected, while the other may be hidden and can be found out only by long careful tests, it would be valuable, indeed, for the employment manager to become acquainted with such correlations as the psychologist may discover: as soon as he becomes aware of the superficially noticeable symptom, he can foresee that the other disposition is most probably present. To give an illustration: in the interest of such measurements of correlations we have studied in the Harvard laboratory the various characteristics of attention and their mutual dependence.[18] We found that typical connections exist between apparently independent features of attention. Persons who have a rather expansive span of attention for acoustical impressions have also a wide span for the visual objects. Persons whose attention is vivid and quick have on the whole the expansive type of attention, while those who attend slowly have a narrow field of attention, and so on. Hence the manifestation of one feature of attention allows us to presuppose without further tests that certain other features may be expected in the particular individual.

The problem of attention, indeed, seems to stand quite in the centre of the field of industrial efficiency. This conviction has grown upon me in my observation of industrial life. The peculiar kind of attention decides more than any mental trait for which economic activity the individual is adapted. The essential point is that such differences of attention cannot be characterized as good or bad; it is not a question of the attentive and of the inattentive mind. One type is not better than another, but is simply different. Two workingmen, not only equally industrious and capable, but also equally attentive, may yet occupy two positions in which they are both complete failures because their attention does not fit the places, and both may become highly efficient as soon as they exchange positions. Their particular types of attention have now found the right places. The one may be disposed to a strong concentration by which everything is inhibited which lies on the mental periphery, the other may have the talent for distributing his attention over a large field, while he is unable to hold it for a long while at one point. If the one industrial activity demands the attentive observation of one little lever or one wheel at one point, while the other demands that half a dozen large machines be simultaneously supervised, all that is necessary is to find the man with the right type of attention for each place. It would be utterly arbitrary to claim that the expansive type of attention is economically more or less valuable than the concentrated type. Both in English and in German we have a long popular series of pamphlets with descriptions of the requirements and conditions for the various occupations to which a boy or a girl may turn, but I have nowhere found any reference to the most essential mental functions such as the particular kind of attention or memory or will. These pamphlets are always cut after the same pattern. Where the detail refers at all to the mental side, it points only to particular knowledge which may be learned in school or trade or work, or to abilities which may be developed by training. But the individual differences which are set by the particular conditions and dispositions of the mind are neglected with surprising uniformity in the vocational literature of all countries. The time seems ripe for at last filling this blank in the consciousness of the nation and in the institutions of the land.

PART II

THE BEST POSSIBLE WORK

PART II

THE BEST POSSIBLE WORK

XIII

LEARNING AND TRAINING

WE have placed our psychotechnical interest at the service of economic tasks. We therefore had to start from the various economic purposes and had to look backward, asking what ways might lead to these goals. All our studies so far were in this sense subordinated to the one task which ought to be the primary one in the economic world, and yet which has been most ignored. The purpose before us was to find for every economic occupation the best-fitted personality, both in the interest of economic success and in the interest of personal development. Individual traits under this point of view become for us the decisive psychological factors, and experimental psychology had to show us a method to determine those personal differences and their relation to the demands for industrial efficiency. This first goal may be reached with all the means of science, as we hope it will be in the future, or everything may be left to unscientific, haphazard methods as in the past: in any case a second task stands before the community, namely, the securing of the best possible work from every man in his place. Indeed, the nation cannot delay the solution of this second problem until the first has been solved in a satisfactory way. We might even say that the answer to the second question is the more important, the less satisfactory the answer to the first is. If every place in the economic world were filled only by those who are perfectly adapted by their mental traits, it would be much less difficult to get efficient work from every one. The fact that so many misfits are at work makes it such an urgent necessity to find ways and means by which the efficiency can be heightened.

It must be acknowledged, however, that the problem of the best work is not quite such a clear one as that of the best man. From various standpoints a different answer may be given to the question which kind of work is the best. A capitalistic, profit-seeking egotism may consider the quickest performance, or, if differences of quality are involved, the most skillful performance, the only desirable end. The social reformers, on the other hand, may consider the best work that which combines the greatest and best possible output with the highest possible saving of the organism and the fullest development of the personality. We have emphasized from the start that the practical psychologist as such has not the right to give a decision upon problems of social civilization. He has to accept the economic tasks from the community for which he is working and his impartial service commences only when the goals have been determined. It is not his share to select the ends, but simply to determine the means after the valuable ends have been chosen. As a psychological scientist he has not the right to enter into the arena of different social party fights. Yet we find after all a broad region which seems rather untouched by any conflict of reasonable opinions. A reckless capitalism on the one side and a feeble sentimentality on the other side may try to widen or to narrow the boundaries of this region, but taken all together, a vigorous healthy nation which is eagerly devoted to its work is on the whole in agreement as to the essential economic demands for efficient labor.

Experience, to be sure, shows that great changes in the conditions of work can never enter into the history of civilization without certain disturbances, and that opposition must therefore necessarily arise in certain groups even against such changes as are undoubtedly improvements and advances from the point of view of the whole nation. Such dissatisfaction arose when the factory system was introduced, and it is only natural that some irritation should accompany the introduction of psychological improvements in the methods of work, inasmuch as not a few wage-earners may at first have to lose their places because a small number of men will under the improved conditions be sufficient for the performance of tasks which needed many before. But the history of economics has clearly shown that from the point of view of the whole community such an apparent disturbance has always been only temporary. If the psychologists succeed in fundamentally improving the conditions of labor, the increased efficiency of the individual will promote such an enriched and vivified economic life that ultimately an increase in the number of laborers needed will result. The inquiry into the possible psychological contributions to the question of reinforced achievement must not be deterred by the superficial objection that in one or another industrial concern a dismissal of wage-earners might at first result. Psychotechnics does not stand in the service of a party, but exclusively in the service of civilization.

To begin at the beginning, we may start from the commonplace that every form of economic labor in the workshop and in the factory, in the field and in the mine, in the store and in the office, must first be learned. How far do the experiments of the psychologist offer suggestions for securing the most economic method of learning practical activities? Bodily actions in the service of economic work are taught and learned in hundreds of thousands of places. It is evident that one method of teaching must reach the goal more quickly and more reliably than another. Some methods of teaching must therefore be economically more advantageous, and yet on the whole the methods of teaching muscular work are essentially left to chance. It is indeed not difficult to observe how factory workers or artisans have learned the same complex motion according to entirely different methods. The result is that they carry out the various partial movements in a different order, or with different auxiliary motions, or in different positions, or in a different rhythm, or with different emphasis, simply because they imitate different teachers, and because no norm, no certainty as to the best methods for the teaching, has been determined. But the process of learning is still more fluctuating and still more dependent upon chance than the process of teaching. The apprentice approaches the instruction in any chance way, and the beginner usually learns even the first steps with a psychophysical attitude which is left to accident. An immense waste of

145

energy and a quite anti-economic training in unfit movements is the necessary result.

The learning of the elements of school knowledge in the classroom in earlier times proceeded after exactly such chance methods. Any one who knew how to read, write, and calculate felt himself prepared to pour reading, writing, and arithmetic into the unprotected children. Methods which are based on scientific examination of the psychophysical process of reading and writing were not at the disposal of the schools, and exact results from comparative studies of pedagogical methods had not been secured. The last few decades have created an entirely new foundation for enlightened school work. The experimental investigations of pedagogical psychology have determined exactly how the consciousness of the child reacts on the various methods of teaching and have built up a real systematic economic learning. All which was left to dilettantic caprice has been transformed into more or less definite standard forms. For instance, the old scheme of teaching reading by the alphabet method is practically eliminated from our modern schools. It is clear that this learning of the names of the single letters as a starting-point for the reading of words was not only a wasting of time and energy, but an actual disturbance in the development of the reading process in the older generation. As those names of the letters do not occur at all in the words to be read, but only their sounds, what had been learned in seeing the single letters had to be inhibited in pronouncing the whole word. It seems not too much to say that the learning of industrial activities on the whole still stands on the level of such alphabet methods, and this cannot be otherwise, as the real problem, namely, the systematic investigation of the psychophysical activities involved, has never been brought into the psychological laboratory.

The pedagogical experiment has shown clearly enough that the subjective feeling of easier or quicker learning may be entirely unreliable and misleading. If the task is to learn a page by heart, we may proceed after many different methods. We may learn very small fractions of the text, repeating only a few words, or we may read whole paragraphs every time; we may repeat the whole material again and again, or we may put in long periods of rest after a few repetitions; we may frequently recite it from memory and have some one to prompt us; we may give our attention especially to the meaning of the words, or merely to the sounds, or we may introduce any number of similar variations. Now the careful experiment shows that of two such methods one which appears to us the better and more appropriate in learning, perhaps even as the easier and more comfortable, may prove itself the less efficient one in the practical result. The psychology of learning, which won its success by introducing meaningless syllables as experimental material, has slowly determined the most reliable methods for impressing knowledge on memory. Where such results have once been secured, it would surely be a grave mistake simply to stick to the methods of so-called common sense and to leave it to the caprice of the individual teacher to decide what method of learning he will suggest to his pupils. The best method is always the only one which should be considered. The psychology of economic work must aim toward similar goals. We must secure a definite knowledge as to the methods by which a group of movements can best be learned. We must understand what value is to be attached to the repetitions and to the pauses, to the imitations and to the special combinations of movements, to the exercise in parts of the movements, to the rhythm of the work, and to many similar influences which may shape the learning process.

The simplest aspect, that of the mere repetition of the movement, has frequently been examined by psychophysicists. The real founder of experimental psychology, Fechner, showed the way; he performed fatiguing experiments with lifted dumb-bells. Then came the time in which the laboratories began to make a record of the muscular activities with the help of the ergograph, an instrument with which the movements of the arm and the fingers can easily be registered on the smoked surface of a revolving drum. The subtlest variations of the activity, the increase and decrease of the psychomotor impulse, the mental fatigue, can be traced exactly in such graphic records. This psychomotor side of the process, and not the mere muscle activity as such, is indeed the essential factor which should interest us. The results of exercise are a training of the central apparatus of the brain and not of the muscular periphery. The further development of those experiments soon led to complex questions, which referred not only to the mere change in the motor efficiency, but to the learning of particular groups of movements and to the influences on the exactitude and reliability of the movements. The purely mental factors of the will-impulse, especially the consciousness of the task, came into the foreground. These experiences of the scientists concerning the influences of training, the mechanization of repetition, and the automatization of movements have been thoroughly discussed by a brilliant political economist [19] as an explana-

149

tion of certain industrial facts, but they have not yet practically influenced life in the factory.

The nearest approach from the experimental side to the study of the effect of training in actual industrial tasks may be found in certain laboratory investigations which refer to the learning of telegraphing, typewriting, and so on. For instance, we have a careful study [20] of the progress made in learning telegraphy, both as to the transmitting of the telegrams by the key movement and the receiving of the telegrams by the ear. It was found that the rapidity of transmitting increases more rapidly and more uniformly than the rapidity of receiving. But while the curve of the latter rises more slowly and more irregularly, it finally reaches the greater height. The ability in transmitting, represented by a graphic record, shows an ascent which corresponds to the typical, steady curve of training. In the receiving curve, on the other hand, we find not far from the beginning a characteristic period during which no progress whatever can be noticed, and this is also repeated at a later stage. The psychological analysis shows that the increase of ability in the receiving of telegrams depends upon the development of a complex system of psychophysical habits. The periods in which the curve does not ascend represent stages of training in which the elementary habits are almost completely formed, but have not become sufficiently automatic. The attention is therefore not yet ready to start habits of a higher order. The lowest correlation refers to the single letters, after that to the syllables and words. As soon as the apprentice has reached this point, he stops, because he must learn to master more and more new words until his telegraphic vocabulary is large enough to make it possible for him to turn his consciousness to whole groups of words at once. Only when this new habit has been made automatic by a training of several months can he advance to a level at which whole groups of words are perceived as telegraphic units. A time follows in which this mastery of whole phrases advances rapidly, until a new period of rest comes, from which, only after years and often quite suddenly, a last new ascent can be noticed. Instead of concentrating the attention with conscious strain on single phrases, the operator progresses to a perfect liberty in which whole sentences are understood automatically.

We also have a model experimental research into the psychological conditions of learning in the case of writing on a typewriter.[21] By electrical connections between the typewriting machine and a system of levers which registered their movements on the rotating drum of a kymograph, each striking of a key, each completion of a word, or of a line, could be recorded in exact time-relations. Each glance at the copy was also registered. It was found that the process of learning consisted first of a continuous simplification of the cumbersome methods with which the beginner commences. A steady elimination of unfit movements, a selection, a reorganization, and finally, a combination of psychophysical acts to impulses of higher order, could be traced exactly. Here, too, the curve of learning at first rises quickly and then more and more slowly. Of course the usual fluctuations in the growth of the ability can also be found, and above all the irregular periods of rest in which the learning itself does not progress, for some of these so-called plateaus which lie between the end of one ascent and the beginning of the next may cover a month and more. At the beginning we have the elementary association between the single letter and the position of the corresponding key, but soon an immediate connection between the visual impression of the whole syllable or the whole word and the total group of movements necessary to strike the keys for it is developed. The more the ability grows, the more these psychical impulses of higher order become organized without conscious intention.

LEARNING AND TRAINING

The study shows that this development of higher habits has already begun before the lower habits are fully settled.

How far the special training involves at the same time a general training which could be of advantage for other kinds of labor has not yet been studied at all with reference to industrial technique. There we are still completely dependent upon certain experiences in the field of experimental pedagogy, and upon certain statistics, for instance, in the textile industry. Many patient investigations, with every independent group of apparatus and machines, may be necessary before psychotechnics will be able to supply industry with reliable advice for teaching and learning. Nor have we the least right hastily to carry over the results from one group of movements to another. Even where superficially a certain similarity between the technical factors exists, the psychophysical conditions may be essentially different. In the two cases mentioned, for instance, telegraphing and typewriting, the chief factor seems the same, as in both cases the aim is to make the quickest possible finger movements for purposes of signals; and yet it is not surprising that the development of the ability from the beginnings to the highest mastery is rather unlike, as all the movements in telegraphing are performed with the same finger, while in typewriting the chief trait is the organization of groups from the impulses to all ten fingers. At least it is certain that learning always means far more than a mere facilitation of the movement by mechanical repetition, and this is true of the simplest handling of the tools in the workshop, of the movements at the machine in the factory, and of the most complex performances at the subtlest instruments. The chief factor in the development is always the organization of the impulses by which the reactions which are at first complicated become simplified, later mechanized, and finally synthesized into a higher group which becomes subordinated to one simple psychical impulse. The most reliable and psychophysically most economic means for this organization will have to be studied in the economic psychological laboratories of the future for every particular technique. Then only can the enormous waste of psychical energy resulting from haphazard methods be brought to an end.

A problem which is still too little considered in industrial life is the mutual interference of acquired technical activities. If one connected series of movements is well trained by practice, does it become less firmly fixed, if another series is studied in which the same beginning is connected with another path of discharge? I approached this psychophysical question of learning by experiments which I carried on for a long while with variations of ordinary habits of daily life, asking whether a habit associated with a certain sensory stimulus can function automatically while dispositions for a different habit, previously acquired, remain in the psychophysical system. For instance, I was accustomed to carry my watch in my left-hand vest pocket. For a week I carried it in the right-hand pocket of my trousers and recorded every case in which I first automatically made the movement to the vest. After some time the movement to the right-hand pocket became entirely automatic. When it was sufficiently fixed, I again put the watch in the left-hand vest pocket and recorded how often I unconsciously grasped at the right side when I wanted to see what time it was. As soon as the vest pocket movement had again become fixed, I went back to the right-hand trousers pocket. And so I alternated for a long while, always changing only after reaching complete automatism. But the results in this case and in other similar experiments which I carried on showed that the new automatic connection did not extinguish the after effects of the previous habit. With every new change the number of wrong movements became smaller and smaller, and finally a point was reached at which the dispositions for both movements were equally developed so that no wrong movements occurred when the watch was put into the new position.[22]

This problem has been followed up very recently in a valuable investigation at Columbia University,[23] in which various habits of typewriting and of card-sorting were acquired and studied in their mutual interference. These very careful experiments also show that when two opposing associations are alternately practiced, they have an interference effect on each other, but that the interference grows less and less as the practice effect becomes greater. The interference effect is gradually overcome and both opposing associations become automatic, so that either of them can be called up independently without the appearance of the other. Many details of the research suggest that this whole group of interference problems deserves the most careful attention by those who would practically profit from increased industrial efficiency.

Finally, in the experimental study of the problem of technical learning, we cannot ignore the many side influences which may hasten or delay, improve or disturb, the acquisition of industrial skill. In the Harvard laboratory, for instance, we are at present engaged in an investigation which deals with the influence of feelings on the rapidity with which new movement coördinations are mastered.[24] In order to have unlimited comparable material a very simple technical performance is required, namely, the distribution of the 52 playing-cards into 52 boxes. Labels on the boxes indicate changing combinations for the distribution to be learned. We examine, on the one side, the influence of feelings of comfort or of discomfort on the learning of the new habit, these feeling states being produced by external conditions, such as pleasant or unpleasant sounds, odors, and so on. On the other side we trace the effects of those feelings which arise during the learning process itself, such as feelings of satisfaction with progress, or disappointment, or discomfort, or disgust or joy in the activity.

XIV

THE ADJUSTMENT OF TECHNICAL TO PSYCHICAL CONDITIONS

TEACHING and learning represent only the preliminary problem. The fundamental question remains, after all, how the work is to be done by those who have learned it in accordance with the customs of the economic surroundings and who are accordingly already educated and trained for it. What can be done to eliminate everything which diminishes and decreases efficiency, and what remains to be done to reinforce it. Such influences are evidently exerted by the external technical conditions, by variations of the activity itself, and by the play of the psychical motives and counter-motives. It must seem as if only this last factor would belong in the realm of psychology, but the technical conditions, of which the machine itself is the most important part, and the bodily movements also have manifold relations to the psychical life. Only as far as these relations prevail has the psychologist any reason to study the problem. The purely physical and economic factors of technique do not interest him at all, but when a technical arrangement makes a psychophysical achievement more difficult or more easy, it belongs in the sphere of the psychologist, and just this aspect of the work may become of greatest importance for the total result. In all three of these directions, that is, with reference to the technical, to the physiological, and to the purely psychical, the scientific management movement has prepared the way. The engineers of scientific management recognized, at least, that no part of the industrial process is indifferent; even the apparently most trivial activity, the slightest movement of arm or hand or leg, became the object of their exact measurement. The stopwatch which measures every movement in fractions of a second has become the symbol of this new economic period. As long as special psychological experiments in the service of industrial psychology are still so exceptional, it may, indeed, be acknowledged that the practical experiments in the service of scientific management have come nearest to the solution of these special psychotechnical problems.

To proceed from without toward the centre, we may begin our review with the physical technique of the working conditions and its relations to the mind. The history of technique shows on every page this practical adjustment of external labor conditions to the psychophysical necessities and psychophysical demands. No machine with which a human being is to work can survive in the struggle for technical existence, unless it is to a certain degree adapted to the human nerve and muscle system and to man's possibilities of perception, of attention, of memory, of feeling, and of will. Industrial technique with its restless improvements has always been subordinated to this postulate. Every change which made it possible for the workingman to secure equal effects with smaller effort or to secure greater or better effects with equal effort counted as an economic gain, which was welcome to the market. For instance, throughout the history of industry we find the fundamental tendency to transpose all activities from the great muscles to the small muscles. Any activity which is performed with the robust muscles of the shoulder when it can be done with the lower arm, or labor which is demanded from the muscles of the lower arm when it can just as well be carried out by the fingers, certainly involves a waste of psychophysical energy. A stronger psychophysical excitement is necessary in order to secure the innervation of the big muscles in the central nervous system. This difference in the stimulation of the various muscle groups has been of significant consequence for the differentiation of work throughout the development of mankind.[25]

THE ADJUSTMENT OF CONDITIONS

Labor with the large muscles has, for these psychophysical reasons, never been easily combined with the subtler training of the finer muscles. Hence a social organization which obliged the men to give their energy to war and the hunt, both, in primitive life, functions of the strongest muscles, made it necessary for the domestic activities, which are essentially functions of the small muscles, to be carried out by women. The whole history of the machine demonstrates this economic tendency to make activities dependent upon those muscles which presuppose the smallest psychophysical effort. It is not only the smaller effort which gives economic advantage to the stimulation of the smaller muscles, but the no less important circumstance that the psychophysical after-effect of their central excitement exerts less inhibition than the after-effect of the brain excitement for the big muscles.

But we must not overlook another feature in the development of technique. The machines have been constantly transformed in the direction which made it possible to secure the greatest help from the natural coördination of bodily movements. The physiological organization and the psychophysical conditions of the nervous system make it necessary that the movement impulses flow over into motor side channels and thus produce accessory effects without any special effort. If a machine is so constructed that these natural accessory movements must be artificially and intentionally suppressed, it means, on the one side, a waste of available psychophysical energy, and on the other side it demands a useless effort in order to secure this inhibition. The industrial development has moved toward both the fructification of those side impulses and the avoidance of these inhibitions. It has adjusted itself practically to the natural psychical conditions. Ultimately it is this tendency which shaped the technical apparatus for the economic work until the muscle movements could become rhythmical. The rhythmical activity necessarily involves a psychophysical saving and this saving has been instinctively secured throughout the history of civilization. All rhythm contains a repetition of movement without making a real repetition of the psychophysical impulse necessary. In the rhythmical activity a large part of the first excitement still serves for the second, and the second for the third. Inhibitions fall away and the mere after-effect of each stimulus secures a great saving for the new impulse. The history of the machine even indicates that the newer technical development not only found the far-reaching division of labor already in the workshops of

162

earlier centuries, but a no less far-reaching rhythmization of the labor in fine adaptation to the needs of the psychophysical organism, long before the appearance of the machines. The beginnings of the machine period frequently showed nothing but an imitation of the rhythmical movements of man.[26] To be sure, the later improvements of the machine have frequently destroyed that original rhythm of man's movement, as the movement itself, especially in the electric machines, has become so quick that the subjective rhythmical experience has been lost. Moreover, the rhythmical horizontal and vertical movements were for physical reasons usually replaced by uniform circular movements. But even the most highly developed machine demands human activity, for instance, for the supplying with material; and this again has opened new possibilities for the adjustment of technical mechanism to the economic demand for rhythmical muscle activity. The growth of technical devices has thus been constantly under the control of psychological demands, in spite of the absence of systematic psychological investigations. But the decisive factor was, indeed, that these psychological motives always remained in the subconsciousness of civilization. The improvements were consciously referred to the machine as such, however much the practical success was really influenced by the degree of its adjustment to the mental conditions of the workingmen. The new movements of scientific management and of experimental psychology aim toward bringing this adaptation consciously into the foreground and toward testing and studying systematically what technical variations can best suit the psychophysical status of man.

Those who are familiar with the achievements of scientific management remember that by no means only the complicated procedures on a high level are in question. The successes are often the most surprising where the technique is old, and where it might have been imagined that the experiences of many centuries would have secured through mere common sense the most effective performance. The best-known case is perhaps that of the masons, which one of the leaders of the scientific management movement has studied in all its details.[27] The movements of the builders and the tools which they use were examined with scientific exactitude and slowly reshaped under the point of view of psychology and physiology. The total result was that after the new method 30 masons completed without greater fatigue what after the old methods it would have taken 100 masons to do, and that the total expense for the building was reduced to less than a half in spite of the steady increase of the wages of the laborers. For this purpose it was necessary that exact measurements be made of the height at which the bricks were lying and of the height of the wall on which they must be laid, and of the number of bricks which should be carried to the masons at once. He studied how the trowel should be shaped and how the mortar should be used and how the bricks should be carried to the bricklayers. In short, everything which usually is left to tradition, to caprice, and to an economy which looks out only for the most immediate saving, was on the basis of experiments of many years replaced by entirely new means and tools, where nothing was left to arbitrariness. Yet these changes did not demand any invention or physically or economically new ideas, but merely a more careful adaptation of the apparatus to the psychological energies of the masons. The new arrangement permitted a better organization of the necessary bodily movements, fatigue was diminished, the accessory movements were better fructified, fewer inhibitions were necessary, a better playing together of the psychical energies was secured.

The students of scientific management stepped still lower in the scale of economic activity. There is no more ordinary productive function than shoveling. Yet in great establishments the shoveling of coal or of dirt may represent an economically very important factor. It seems that up to the days of scientific management, no one really looked carefully into the technical conditions under which the greatest possible economic effect might be reached. Now the act of shoveling was approached with the carefulness with which a scholar turns to any subtle process in his laboratory. The brilliant originator of the scientific management movement, who carried out these investigations [28] in the great Bethlehem Steel Works, where hundreds of laborers had to shovel heavy iron ore or light ashes, found that the usual chance methods involve an absurd economic waste. The burden was sometimes so heavy that rapid fatigue developed and the movements became too slow, or the lifted mass was so light that the larger part of the laborer's energies remained unused. In either case the final result of the day's work must be anti-economic. He therefore tested with carefully graded experiments what weight ensured the most favorable achievement by a strong healthy workingman. The aim was to find the weight which would secure with well-arranged pauses the maximum product in one day without over-fatigue. As soon as this weight was determined, a special set of shovels had to be constructed for every particular kind of material. The laborers were now obliged to operate with 10 different kinds of shovels, each of such a size that the burden always remained an average of 21 pounds for any kind of material. The following step was an exact determination of the most favorable rapidity and the most perfect movement of shoveling, the best distribution of pauses, and so on, and the final outcome was that only 140 men were needed where on the basis of the old plan about 500 laborers had been engaged. The average workingman who had previously shoveled 16 tons of material, now managed 59 tons without greater fatigue. The wages were raised by two thirds and the expenses for shoveling a ton of material were decreased one half. This calculation of expenses included, of course, a consideration of the increased cost for tools and for the salaries of the scientific managers.

Whoever visits factories in which the new system has been introduced by real specialists must be surprised, indeed, by the great effects which often result from the better psychophysical adaptation of the simplest and apparently most indifferent tools and means. As far as the complicated machines are concerned, we are accustomed to a steady improvement by the efforts of the technicians and we notice it rather little if the changes in them are introduced for psychological instead of the usual physical reasons. But the fact that even the least complicated and most indifferent devices can undergo most influential improvements, as soon as they are seriously studied from a psychological point of view, remains really a source for surprise. Sometimes no more is needed than a change in the windows or in the electric lamps, by which the light can fall on the work in a psychologically satisfactory way; sometimes long series of experiments have to be made with a simple hammer or knife or table. Often everything must be arranged against the wishes of the workingmen, who feel any deviation from the accustomed conditions as a disturbance which is to be regarded with suspicion. In one concern I heard that the scientific manager became convinced that all the working-chairs for the women were too low and that the laborers therefore had to hold their arms in a psychophysically unfavorable position during the handling of the apparatus. All were strongly opposed to the introduction of higher chairs. The result was that the manager arranged for the chairs to be raised a few millimeters every evening, without the knowledge of the working-women, as soon as the factory was empty. After a few weeks the chairs had reached the right height without those engaged in the work having noticed it at all. The outcome was a decided increase of efficiency.

But the most rational scheme will after all be to prepare for such arrangements of tools and apparatus by systematic experiments in the psychological laboratory. The subtlety of such investigations will lead far beyond the point which is accessible to the attempts of scientific management. Exact experiments on attention, for instance, will have to determine how the various parts of the apparatus are to be distributed best in space if the laborer must keep watch for disturbances at various places. Only the laboratory experiment can find the most favorable speed of the machine or can select the muscles to which the mind can send the most effective impulses. The construction of the machine must then be adapted to such results. In the Harvard laboratory, for instance, a practical question led us to examine which fingers would allow the quickest alternation of key movements.[29] If any two of the ten fingers perform for ten seconds the quickest possible alternation of motion, as in a trill, the experiment can demonstrate exactly the differences between the various combinations of fingers and the individual fluctuations for these differences. With an electrical

169

registration of the movements of the alternating fingers we studied in hundredths of a second the time for the motions of two hands and of fingers of the same hand, in order to adjust the keys of a certain machine to the most favorable impulses.

We approach this group of problems from another side when we test the relations of various kinds of machines to various mental types. Psychologists have studied, for example, the various styles of typewriting machines.[30] From a purely commercial point of view the merits of one or another machine are praised as if they were advantageous for every possible human being. The fact is that such advantages for one may be disadvantages for another on account of differences in the mental disposition. One man may write more quickly on one, another on another machine. As every one knows, the chief difference is that of the keyboard and that of the visible or invisible writing. Machines like the Remington machine work with a shift key; that is, a special key must be pressed when capital letters are to be written. Other machines like the Oliver even demand double shifting, one key for the capital letters, and one for the figures, and so on. On the other hand, machines like the Smith Premier have no shift key, but a double keyboard.

THE ADJUSTMENT OF CONDITIONS

It is evident that both the shift-key arrangement and the double keyboard have their particular psychological advantages.

The single alphabet demands much less from the optical memory, and the corresponding motor inner attitude of consciousness is adjusted to a smaller number of possibilities. But the pressure on the shift key, which goes with the single alphabet, is not only a time-wasting act; from the psychological point of view it is first of all a very strong interruption of the uniform chain of impulses. If the capital and small letters are written for a minute alternatingly with the greatest possible speed, the experiment shows that the number of letters for the machine with the double alphabet is about three times greater than for the machine with simple alphabet and shift key. Both systems accordingly have their psychological advantages and disadvantages. Human beings of distinct visual ideational type or of highly developed motor type will prefer the double alphabet, provided, of course, that the touch system of writing is learned, and this will be especially true if their inner attitude is easily disturbed by interruptions. But those who have a feebly developed optical mental centre and who have small ability for the development of complex motor habits will be more efficient on the machines with the single alphabet, especially if their nervous system is little molested by interruptions and thus undisturbed by the intrusion of the shift key act.

In a similar way the visibility of the writing will be for certain individuals the most valuable condition for quick writing, while for others, who depend less upon visual support, it may mean rather a distraction and an interference with the speediest work. The visible writing attracts the involuntary attention, and thus forces consciousness to stick to that which has been written instead of being concentrated on that which is to be produced by the next writing movements. The operator himself is not aware of this hindrance. On the contrary, the public will always be inclined to prefer the typewriters with visible writing, because by a natural confusion the feeling arises that the production of the letter is somewhat facilitated, when the eye is coöperating, just as in writing with a pen we follow the lines of the written letter. But the situation lies differently in the two cases. When we are writing with a pen, the letter grows under our eyes, while in the machine writing we do not see any part of the letter until the whole movement which produces the single letter is finished. By such a misleading analogy many a man is led to prefer the typewriter with visible writing, while he would probably secure a greater speed with a machine which does not tempt him to attend the completed letters, while his entire attention ought to belong to the following letters.

These last observations point to another psychological aspect of the machine and of the whole technical work, namely, their relations to the impressions of the senses. The so-called dynamogenic experiments of the psychological laboratory have demonstrated what a manifold influence flows from the sense-impressions to the will-impulses. If the muscle contraction of a man's fist is measured, the experiment shows that the strongest possible pressure may be very different when the visual field appears in different colors, or tones of different pitch or different noises are stimulating the ear, and so on. As yet no systematic experiments exist by which such results can be brought into relation to the sense-stimuli which reach the laborer during his technical work. The psychophysical effect of colors and noises has not been fructified at all for industrial purposes. The mere subjective judgment of the working-man himself cannot be acknowledged as reliable in such questions. The laborer, for instance, usually believes that a noise to which he has become accustomed does not disturb him in his work,

173

while experimental results point strongly to the contrary. In a similar way the effect of colored windows may appear indifferent to the workmen, and yet may have considerable influence on his efficiency. Numberless performances in the factory are reactions on certain optical or acoustical or tactual signals. Both the engineer and the workman are satisfied if such a signal is clearly perceivable. The psychological laboratory experiment, however, shows that the whole psychophysical effect depends upon the character of the signal; a more intense light, a quicker change, a higher tone, a larger field of light, a louder noise, or a harder touch may produce a very different kind of reaction.

With a careful time-measurement of the motions, it can often be directly traced how purely technical processes in the machine itself influence and control the whole psychical system of impulses in the man. I observed, in a factory, for instance, the work at a machine which performed most of its functions automatically. It had to hammer fine grooves into small metal plates. A young laborer stood before every such machine, took from a pile, alternately from the right and from the left, the little plates to be serrated, placed them in the machine, turned a lever to bring the hammer into motion, and then removed the serrated plates. The speed of the work was dependent upon the operative, as he determined by his lever movement the instant at which the automatic serrating hammer should be released. The man's activity demanded 9 independent movements. I found that those who worked the most quickly were able to carry out this labor for hours at a uniform rapidity of 4 to $4\frac{1}{2}$ seconds for those 9 movements. But the time-measurement showed that even these fastest workers were relatively slow in the first 5 movements which they made while the machine stood quiet, and that they reached an astonishing quickness of movement in the 4 last actions during which at the same time the serrating hammer in bewildering rapidity was beating on the plate with sharp loud cracks. The hammer reinforced the energy of the young laborers to an effectiveness which could never have been attained by mere voluntary effort.

Often the simplicity or complication of the stimulus may be decisive in importance, and this also holds true where the most elementary reactions are involved, for instance, the mere act of counting which enters into many industrial functions. Experiments carried on in my laboratory [31] have shown that the time needed to count a certain number of units becomes longer

175

as soon as the units themselves become more complicated. Their inner manifoldness exerts a retarding influence on the eye as it moves from one figure to another. A certain psychical inhibition arises; the mind is held back by the complexity of the impression and cannot proceed quickly enough to the next. Psychologically no less important is the demand that the external technical conditions so far as they influence consciousness, should remain as far as possible the same, if the same psychical effect is desired, because then only can a perfectly firm connection between stimulus and movement be formed. In technical life this demand is much sinned against. A typical case is that of the signals for which the engineer on the locomotive has to watch. In the daytime the movable arms of the semaphore indicate by their horizontal, oblique, or vertical position whether the tracks are clear. At nighttime, on the other hand, the same information reaches him by the different colors of the signal lanterns. From a psychical point of view it is probable that the safety of the service would be increased if an unchangeable connection between signal and movement were formed. It would be sufficient for that purpose if the color signals at night were given up and were replaced by horizontal, oblique, or vertical lines of white light or rows of points. Successful experiments of this kind have been carried on by psychologists in the service of this railroad problem.[32]

The interest in all these problems of large concerns, in transportation and factory work and complex industries, ought not to make us overlook the fact that on principle the same problems can be found in the simplest industrial establishment. Even the housewife or the cook destroys economic values if daily she has to spend useless minutes or hours on account of arrangements in the household which are badly adjusted to the psychological conditions. She sacrifices her energy in vain and she wastes her means where she herself is under the illusion of especial economy. Scientific management would perhaps be nowhere so wholesome as in kitchen and pantry, in laundry and cellar, just because here the saving would be multiplied millionfold and the final sum of energy saved and of feeling values gained would be enormous, even if it could not be calculated with the exactitude with which the savings of a factory budget can be proven. The profusion of small attractive devices which automatically perform the economic household labor and disburden the human workers must not hide the fact that the chief activities are still little adjusted to the psychophysical conditions. The situation is similar to that of the masons, whose function has also been performed for thousands of years, and yet which did not find a real adaptation to the psychical factors until a systematic time-measuring study was introduced. A manufacturer who sells an improved pan or mixing-spoon or broom expects success if he brings to the market something the merits of which are evident and make the housewife anticipate a decrease of work or a simplification of work, but the development of scientific management has shown clearly that the most important improvements are just those which are deduced from scientific researches, without at first giving satisfaction to the laborers themselves, until a new habit has been formed.

Perhaps the most frequent technical activity of this simple kind is sewing by hand, which is still entirely left to the traditions of common sense, and yet which is evidently dependent upon the interplay of many psychical factors which demand a subtle adaptation to the psychical conditions. To approach, at least, this field of human labor a careful investigation of the psychophysics of sewing has been started in my laboratory.[33] The sewing work is done, with the left hand supported, and the right hand connected with a system of levers which make a graphic record of every movement on the smoked surface of a revolving drum. For instance, we begin with simple over and over stitches, measuring the time and the character of the right hand movements for 50 stitches under a variety of technical conditions. The first variation refers to the length of the thread. The thread itself, fixed at the needle's eye, varied between 3 feet and 6 inches in length. Other changes refer to the voluntary speed, to the number of stitches, to fatigue, to external stimuli, to attention, to methods of training, and so on, but the chief interest remains centred on the psychical factors. We are still too much at the beginning already to foresee whether it will be possible to draw from these psychophysical experiments helpful conclusions. The four young women engaged in this laboratory research will later extend it to the psychological conditions of work with the various types of sewing-machines.

XV

THE ECONOMY OF MOVEMENT

THE study of the technical aspect of labor can nowhere be separated by a sharp demarcation line from the study of the labor itself as a function of the individual organism. Many problems, indeed, extend in both directions. The student of industrial efficiency is, for instance, constantly led to the question of fatigue. He may consider this fatigue as a function of brain and muscle activity and discuss it with reference to the psychophysical effort, but he is equally interested in the question of how far the apparatus or the machine or the accessory conditions of the work might be changed in order to avoid fatigue. The accidents of the electric street railways were regarded as partly related to fatigue. The problem was accordingly how to shorten the working time of the motormen in the interest of the public, but it was soon recognized that the difficulty might also be approached from the mere technical side. Some companies introduced seats which the motormen can use whenever they feel fatigue coming and excellent results have followed this innovation. In our last discussions the technical apparatus stood in the foreground. We may now consider as our real topic the psychophysical activity.

Here, too, the leaders of scientific management have secured some signal successes. Their chief effort in this field was directed toward the greatest possible achievement by eliminating all superfluous movements and by training in those movement combinations which were recognized as the most serviceable ones. We may return to the case of the masons in order to clear up the principle. When Gilbreth began to reform the labor of the mason after scientific principles, he gave his chief interest to the men's motions. Every muscle contraction which was needed to move the brick from the pile in the yard to the final position in the wall was measured with reference to space- and time-relations and the necessary effort. From here he turned to the application of well-known psychophysical principles. A movement is less fatiguing and therefore economically most profitable if it occurs in a direction in which the greatest possible use of gravitation can be made. If both hands have to act at the same time, the labor can be carried out most quickly and with the smallest effort if corresponding muscle groups are at work and this means if symmetrical movements are performed. If unequal movements have to be made simultaneously, the effort will become smaller if they are psychically bound together by a common unified impulse. The distance which has to be overcome by hands, arms, or feet must be brought to a minimum for each partial movement. Most important, however, is this rule. If a definite combination of movements has been determined as economically most suitable, this method must be applied without any exception from the beginning of the learning. The point is to train from the start those impulse combinations which can slowly lead to the quickest and best work. The usual method is the opposite. Generally the beginner learns to produce from the beginning work which is as good and correct as possible. In order to produce such qualitatively good results at an early stage, it is left to him to choose any groups of movements which happen to be convenient to him. Then these become habitual, and as soon as he tries to go on to quicker work, these chance habits hinder him in his progress. The movements which may be best suited for fair production by a beginner may be entirely unsuited for really quick work, such as would be expected from an experienced man. The laborer must replace the first habits which he has learned by a new set, instead of starting in the first place with motions which can be continued until the highest point of efficiency has been reached, even if this involves rather a poor showing at the beginning. A final maximum rapidity must be secured from the start by the choice of those motions which have been standardized by careful experiments.

It is also psychophysically important to demand that the movements shall not be suddenly stopped, if that can be avoided. Any interruption of a movement presupposes a special effort of the will which absorbs energy, and after the interruption a new start must be made of which the same is true. On the other hand, if chains of movements become habitual, the psychophysical effort will be reduced to the minimum, inasmuch as each movement finds its natural end and is not artificially interrupted by will, and at the same time each movement itself becomes a stimulus for the next movement by its accompanying sensations. The traditional method, for instance, demands that a brick be lifted with one hand and a trowel with mortar by the other hand. After that the lifting movement is interrupted, the brick comes to rest in the hand of the mason until the mortar has been spread on and the place prepared for the new brick. Then only begins a new action with the brick. This method was fundamentally changed. The laborers learned to swing the brick with one hand from the pack to the wall and at the same time to distribute the mortar over the next brick with the other hand. This whole complex movement is of course more difficult and demands a somewhat longer period of learning, but as soon as it is learned an extreme saving of psychophysical energy and a correspondingly great economic gain is secured. The newly trained masons are not even allowed to gather up with the trowel any mortar which falls to the floor, because it was found that the loss of mortar is economically less important than the waste of psychophysical energy in bending down.

Whoever has once schooled his eye to observe the limitless waste of human motions and psychophysical efforts in social life has really no difficulty in perceiving all this at every step. This ability to recognize possible savings of impulse may be brought to a certain virtuosity. Gilbreth, one of the leaders of the new movement, seems to be such a virtuoso. When he was in London, there was pointed out to him in the Japanese British Exhibition a young girl who worked so quickly that there at least he would find a rhythm of finger movement which could not any further be improved. In an exhibition booth the woman attached advertisement labels to boxes with phenomenal rapidity. Gilbreth watched her for a little

184

while and found that she was able to manage 24 boxes in 40 seconds. Then he told the young girl that she was doing it wrongly, and that she ought to try a new way which he showed her. At the first attempt, she disposed of 24 boxes in 26 seconds and at the second trial in 20 seconds. She did not have to make more effort for it, but simply had fewer movements to make. If such economic gain can be secured with little exertion in the simplest processes, it cannot be surprising that in the case of more complex and more advanced technical work which involves highly skilled labor, a careful psychophysical study of motions must bring far-reaching economic improvements.

Yet the more important steps will have to be guided by special experimental investigations, and here the psychological laboratory must undertake the elaboration of the details. Only the systematic experiment can determine what impulses can be released at the least expense of energy and with the greatest exactitude of the motor effect. Investigations on the psychophysics of movement and the influences which lead toward making the movement too large or too small have played an important rôle in the psychological laboratories for several decades. It was recognized early that the mistakes which are made in reproducing a movement may spring from two different sources.

THE BEST POSSIBLE WORK

They result partly from an erroneous perception or memory of the movement carried out, and partly from the inability to realize the movement intention. One series of investigations was accordingly devoted to the studies of those sensations and perceptions by which we become aware of the actual movement. Everything which accentuates these sensations must lead to an overestimation of the motion, and the outcome is that the movement is made too small. The concentration of attention, therefore, has the effect of reducing the actual motion, and the same influence must result from any resistance which is not recognized as such and hence is not subtracted in the judgment of the perceiver. Another series of researches was concerned with the inner attitude which causes a certain external movement effect and which may lead to an unintended amount of movement as soon as the weight to be lifted is erroneously judged upon. Closely related studies, finally, deal with a mistake which enters when the movement is reproduced from memory after a certain time. The exactitude of a simple arm movement seems to increase in the first ten seconds, then rapidly to decrease. The emotional attitude, too, is of importance for the reproduction of a movement. I trained myself in making definite extensor and flexor movements of the arm until I was able to reproduce them under normal conditions with great exactitude. In experiments extending over many months, which were carried on through the changing emotional attitudes of daily life, the exact measurement showed that both groups of movements became too large in states of excitement and too small in states of fatigue. But in a state of satisfaction and joy the extensor movement became too large, the flexor movement too small, and *vice versa,* in unpleasant emotional states the flexor movement was too strong and the extensor movement too weak.[34]

We have a very careful investigation into the relations between rapidity of movement and exactitude.[35] The subjects had to perform a hand movement simultaneously with the beat of a metronome, the beats of which varied between 20 and 200 in the minute. In general the accuracy of the movement decreases as the rapidity increases, but the descent is not uniform. Motions in the rhythm of 40 to the minute were on the whole just as exact as those in the rhythm of 20, and, on the other hand movements in the rhythm of 200 almost as accurate as those of 140 to the minute. Thus we have a lower limit below which decrease of rapidity does not increase the accuracy any further, and an upper limit beyond which a further increase of rapidity brings no additional deterioration. The mistakes of the unskilled left hand increase still more rapidly than the number of movements. If the eyes are closed, the rapid movements are usually too long and the slow ones too short.

An investigation in the Harvard laboratory varied this problem in a direction which brings it still nearer to technical conditions of industry. Our central question was whether the greatest exactitude of rhythmical movement is secured at the same rapidity for different muscle groups.[36] We studied especially rhythmical movements of hand, foot, arm, and head, and studied them, moreover, under various conditions of resistance. The result from 340,000 measured movements was the demonstration that every muscle group has its own optimum of rapidity for the greatest possible accuracy and that the complexity of the movement and the resistance which it finds has most significant influence on the exactitude of the rhythmical achievement. If we abstract at first from the fluctuations around the average value of a particular group of movements and consider only this average itself in its relation to the starting movement which it is meant to imitate, we find characteristic tendencies toward enlargement or reduction dependent upon the rapidity. The right foot, for instance, remained nearest to the original movement at a rapidity of 80 motions in the minute, while the head did the same at about 20. For a hand movement of 14 centimeters, the most favorable rapidity was 120 repetitions in the minute, while for a hand movement of 1 centimeter the average remained nearest to the standard at about 40 repetitions. The mean variation from the average is the smallest for the left foot at 20 to 30 movements, for the right at 160 to 180, for the head at 40, for the larger hand movement at 180, and so on. Investigations of this kind have so far not affected industrial life in the least, but it seems hardly doubtful that a systematic study of the movements necessary for economic work will have to pass through such strictly experimental phases. The essential point, however, will be for the managers of the industrial concerns and the psychological laboratory workers really to come nearer to each other from the start and undertake the work in common, not in the sense that the laboratory is to emigrate to the factory, but in the better sense that definite questions which grow out of the industrial life be submitted to the scientific investigation of the psychologists.

XVI

EXPERIMENTS ON THE PROBLEM OF MONOTONY

THE systematic organization of movements with most careful regard to the psychophysical conditions appeared to us the most momentous aid toward the heightening of efficiency. But even if the superfluous, unfit, and interfering movement impulses were eliminated and the conditions of work completely adjusted to the demands of psychology, there would still remain a large number of possibilities through which productiveness might be greatly decreased, or at least kept far below the possible maximum of efficiency. For instance, even the best adapted labor might be repeated to the point of exhaustion, at which the workman and the work would be ruined. Fatigue and restoration accordingly demand especial consideration. In a similar way emotions may be conditions of stimulation or interference, and no one ought to underestimate the importance of higher motives, intellectual, æsthetic, and moral motives, in their bearing on the psychophysical impulses of the laborer. If these higher demands are satisfied, the whole system gains a new tonus, and if they are disappointed, the irritation of the mental machinery may do more harm than any break in the physical machine at which the man is working. In short, we must still look in various directions to become aware of all the relations between the psychological factors and the economic output. We may begin with one question which plays a large, perhaps too large, rôle in the economic and especially in the popular economic literature. I refer to the problem of monotony of labor.

In the discourses of our time on the lights and shades of our modern industrial life, all seem to agree that the monotony of industrial labor ought to be entered on the debit side of the ledger of civilization. Since the days when factories began to spring up, the accusation that through the process of division of labor the industrial working-man no longer has any chance to see a whole product, but that he has to devote himself to the minutest part of a part, has remained one of the matter-of-course arguments. The part of a part which he has to cut or polish or shape in endless repetition without alteration cannot awake any real interest. This complete division of labor has to-day certainly gone far beyond anything which Adam Smith described, and therefore it now appears undeniable that the method must create a mental starvation which presses down the whole life of the laborer, deprives it of all joy in work, and makes the factory scheme a necessary but from the standpoint of psychology decidedly regrettable evil. I have become more and more convinced that the scientific psychologist is not obliged to endorse this judgment of popular psychology.

To be sure the problem of division of labor, as it appears in the subdivision of manufacture, is intimately connected with many other related questions. It quickly leads to the much larger question of division of labor in our general social structure, which is necessary for our social life with its vocational and professional demands, and which undoubtedly narrows to a certain degree every individual in the completeness of his human desires. No man in modern society can devote himself to everything for which his mind may long. But as a matter of course these large general problems of civilization lie outside of the realm of our present inquiry. In another direction the problem of monotony comes very near to the question of fatigue. But we must see clearly that these two questions are not identical and that we may discuss monotony here without arguing the problem of fatigue. The frequent repetition of the same movement or of the same mental activity certainly may condition an objective fatigue, which may interfere with the economic output, but this is not the real meaning of the problem of monotony. About fatigue we shall speak later. Here we are concerned exclusively with that particular psychological attitude which we know as subjective dislike of uniformity and lack of change in the work. Within these limits the question of monotony is, indeed, frequently misunderstood in its economic significance.

Let us not forget that the outsider can hardly ever judge when work offers or does not offer inner manifoldness. If we do not know and really understand the subject, we are entirely unable to discriminate the subtler inner differences. The shepherd knows every sheep, though the passerby has the impression that they all look alike. This inability to recognize the differences which the man at work feels distinctly shows itself even in the most complicated activities. The naturalist is inclined to fancy that the study of a philologist must be endlessly monotonous, and the philologist is convinced that it must be utterly tiresome to devote one's self a life long to some minute questions of natural science. Only when one stands in the midst of the work is he aware of its unlimited manifoldness, and feels how every single case is somehow different from every other.

THE BEST POSSIBLE WORK

In the situation of the industrial workman, the attention may be directed toward some small differences which can only be recognized after long familiarity with the particular field. Certainly this field is small, as every workman must specialize, but whether he manufactures a whole machine, or only a little wheel, makes no essential difference in the attitude. The attraction of newness is quickly lost also in the case of the most complicated machine. On the other hand, the fact that such a machine has an independent function does not give an independent attraction to the work. Or we might rather say, as far as the work on a whole machine is of independent value, the work of perfecting the little wheel is an independent task also and offers equal value by its own possibilities. Whoever has recognized the finest variations among the single little wheels and has become aware of how they are produced sometimes better, sometimes worse, sometimes more quickly, sometimes more slowly, becomes as much interested in the perfecting of the minute part as another man in the manufacture of the complex machine. It is true that the laborer does not feel interest in the little wheel itself, but in the production of the wheel. Every new movement necessary for it has a perfectly new chance and stands in new relations, which have nothing to do with the repetition. As a matter of course this interest in the always new best possible method of production is still strongly increased where piece-wages are introduced. The laborer knows that the amount of his earning depends upon the rapidity with which he finishes faultless products. Under this stimulus he is in a continuous race with himself, and thus has every reason to prefer the externally uniform and therefore perfectly familiar work to another kind which may bring alternation, but which also brings ever new demands.

For a long while I have tried to discover in every large factory which I have visited the particular job which from the standpoint of the outsider presents itself as the most tiresome possible. As soon as I found it, I had a full frank talk with the man or woman who performed it and earnestly tried to get self-observational comment. My chief aim was to bring out how far the mere repetition, especially when it is continued through years, is felt as a source of discomfort. I may again point to a few chance illustrations. In an electrical factory with many thousands of employees I gained the impression that the prize for monotonous work belonged to a woman who packs incandescent lamps in tissue paper. She wraps them from morning until night, from the first day of the year to the last, and has been doing that for the last 12 years. She performs this packing process at an average rate of 13,000 lamps a day. The woman has reached about 50,000,000 times for the next lamp with one hand and with the other to the little pile of tissue sheets and then performed the packing. Each lamp demands about 20 finger movements. As long as I watched her, she was able to pack 25 lamps in 42 seconds, and only a few times did she need as many as 44 seconds. Every 25 lamps filled a box, and the closing of the box required a short time for itself. She evidently took pleasure in expressing herself fully about her occupation. She assured me that she found the work really interesting, and that she constantly felt an inner tension, thinking how many boxes she would be able to fill before the next pause. Above all, she told me that there is continuous variation. Sometimes she grasps the lamp or paper in a different way, sometimes the packing itself does not run smoothly, sometimes she feels fresher, sometimes less in the mood for the work, and there is always something to observe and something to think about.

This was the trend which I usually found. In some large machine works I sought for a long time before I found the type of labor which seemed to me the most monotonous. I finally settled on a man who was feeding an automatic machine which was cutting holes in metal strips and who simply had to push the strips slowly forward; only when the strip did not reach exactly the right place, he could stop the automatic machine by a lever. He made about 34,000 uniform movements daily and had been doing that for the past 14 years. But he gave me the same account, that the work was interesting and stimulating, while he himself made the impression of an intelligent workingman. At the beginning, he reported, the work had sometimes been quite fatiguing, but later he began to like it more and more. I imagined that this meant that at first he had to do the work with full attention and that the complex movement had slowly become automatic, allowing him to perform it like a reflex movement and to turn his thoughts to other things. But he explained to me in full detail that this was not the case, that he still feels obliged to devote his thoughts entirely to the work at hand, and that he is able only under these conditions to bring in the daily wage which he needs for his family, as he is paid for every thousand holes. But he added especially that it is not only the wage which satisfies him, but that he takes decided pleasure in the activity itself.

On the other hand, I not seldom found wage-earners, both men and women, who seemed to have really interesting and varied activities and who nevertheless complained bitterly over the monotonous, tiresome factory labor. I became more and more convinced that the feeling of monotony depends much less upon the particular kind of work than upon the special disposition of the individual. It cannot be denied that the same contrast exists in the higher classes of work. We find school-teachers who constantly complain that it is intolerably monotonous to go on teaching immature children the rudiments of knowledge, while other teachers with exactly the same task before them are daily inspired anew by the manifoldness of life in the classroom. We find physicians who complain that one case in their practice is like another, and judges who despair because they always have to deal with the same petty cases, while other judges and physicians feel clearly that every case offers something new and that the repetition as such is neither conspicuous nor disagreeable. We find actors who feel it a torture to play the same rôle every evening for several weeks, and there are actors who, as one of the most famous actresses assured me after the four hundredth performance of her star rôle, repeat their parts many hundred times with undiminished interest, because they feel that they are always speaking to new audiences. It seems not impossible that this individual difference might be connected with deeper-lying psychophysical conditions. I approached the question, to be sure, with a preconceived theory. I fancied that certain persons had a finer, subtler sense for differences than others and that they would recognize a manifoldness of variations where the others would see only uniformity. In that I silently presupposed that the perception of the uniformity must be something disturbing and disagreeable and the recognition of variations something which stimulates the mind pleasantly. But when I came to examine the question experimentally, I became convinced that such a hypothesis is erroneous, and if I interpret the results correctly, I should say that practically the opposite relation exists. Those who recognize the uniformities readily are not the ones who are disturbed by them.

I proceeded in the following way. To make use of a large number of subjects accustomed to intelligent self-observation, I made the first series of experiments with the regular students in my psychology lecture course in Harvard University. Last winter I had more than four hundred men students in psychology who all took part in that introductory series. The task which I put before

them in a number of variations was this: I used
lists of words of which half, or one more or less
than half, belonged to one single conceptional
group. There were names of flowers, or cities,
or poets, or parts of the body, or wild animals,
and so on. The remaining words of the list, on
the other hand, were without inner connection and
without similarity. The similar and the dissimilar
words were mixed. The subjects listened to such
a list of words and then had to decide without
counting from the mere impression whether the
similar words were more or equally or less numerous than the dissimilar words. In other experiments the arrangement was that two different
lists were read and that in the two lists a larger
or smaller number of words were repeated from
the first list. Here, too, the subjects had to decide
from the mere impression whether the repeated
words were in the majority or not. In every experiment the judgment referred to those words which
belonged to the same group and which were in this
sense uniform, or to the repeated words, and it
had to be stated with reference to them whether
their number was larger, equal to, or smaller than
the different words. If all replies had been correct,
the judgment would have been 40 per cent equal,
30 per cent smaller, and 30 per cent larger, as
they were arranged in perfect symmetry. As soon

as I had the results from the students, we figured out for every one what number he judged equal, smaller, or greater. Then we divided the equal judgments by 2 and added half of them to the larger and half to the smaller judgments. In this way we were enabled by one figure to characterize the whole tendency of the individual. We found that in the whole student body there was a tendency to underestimate the number of the similar or of the repeated words. The majority of my students had a stronger impression from the varying objects than from those which were in a certain sense equal. Yet this tendency appeared in very different degrees and for about a fourth of the participants the opposite tendency prevailed. They received a stronger impression from the uniform ideas.

I had coupled with these experimental tests a series of questions, and had asked every subject to express with fullest possible self-analysis his practical attitude to monotony in life. Every one had to give an account whether in the small habits of life he liked variety or uniform repetition. He was asked especially as to his preferences for or against uniformity in the daily meals, daily walks, and so on. Furthermore he had to report how far he is inclined to stick to one kind of work or to alternate his work, how far he welcomes the idea that vocational work may bring repetition, and so on. And finally I tried to bring the results of these self-observations into relation with the results of those experiments. It was here that the opposite of the hypothesis which I had presupposed suggested itself to me with surprising force. I found that just the ones who perceive the repetition least hate it most, and that those who have a strong perception of the uniform impressions and who overestimate their number are the ones who on the whole welcome repetition in life.

As soon as I had reached this first experimental result, I began to see how it might harmonize with known psychological facts. Some years ago a Hungarian psychologist[37] showed by interesting experiments that if a series of figures is exposed to the eye for a short fraction of a second, equal digits are seen only once, and he came to the conclusion that equal impressions in such a series inhibit each other. In the Harvard laboratory we varied these experiments by eliminating the spatial separation of those numbers. In our experiments the digits did not stand side by side, but followed one another very quickly in the same place.[38] Similar experiments we made with colors and so on. Here, too, we found that quickly succeeding equal or very similar impressions have a tendency to inhibit each other or to fuse with each other. Where such an inhibition occurs, we probably ought to suppose that the perception of the first impression exhausts the psychical disposition for this particular mental experience. The psychophysical apparatus becomes for a moment unable to arouse the same impression once more.

The above described new experiments suggest to me that this inhibition of equal or similar impressions is found unequally developed in different individuals. They possess a different tendency to temporary exhaustion of psychophysical dispositions. There are evidently persons who after they have received an impression are unable immediately to seize the same impression again. Their attention and their whole inner attitude fails. But there are evidently other persons for whom, on the contrary, the experience of an impression is a kind of inner preparation for arousing the same or a similar impression. In their case the psychophysical dispositions become stimulated and excited, and therefore favor the repetition. If, as in our experiments, the task is simply to judge the existence of equal or similar impressions without any strain of attention, the one group of persons must underestimate the number of the equal impressions because many words are simply inhibited in their minds and remain neglected, the other groups of persons must from their mental dispositions overestimate the number of similar words. From here we have to take one step more. If these two groups of persons have to perform a task in which it is necessary that not a single member of a series of repetitions be overlooked, it is clear that the two groups must react in a very different way. Now a perfect perception of every single member is forced on them. Those who grasp equal impressions easily, and who are prepared beforehand for every new repetition by their inner dispositions, will follow the series without strain and will experience the repetition itself with true satisfaction. On the other hand, those in whom every impression inhibits the readiness to receive a repetition, and whose inner energy for the same experience is exhausted, must feel it as a painful and fatiguing effort if they are obliged to turn their attention to one member after another in a uniform series. This mental torture is evidently the displeasure which such individuals call the dislike of monotony in their work. Whether this theoretical view is correct, we have to determine by future studies. In our Harvard laboratory we have now proceeded from such preparatory mass experiments to subtle investigations on a small number of persons well trained in psychological self-observation with whom the conditions of the experiment can be varied in many directions.[39]

It would seem probable that such experiments might also win psychotechnical significance. A short series of tests which would have to be adapted to the special situations, and which for the simple wage-earner would have to be much easier than those sketched above, would allow it to be determined beforehand whether an individual will suffer from repetition in work. Even if we abstract from arguments of social reform and consider exclusively the economic significance, it must seem important that labor which involves much repetition be performed by men and women whose mental dispositions favor an easy grasp of successive uniform impressions. Experimentation could secure the selection of the fit workmen and the complaint of monotony would disappear. The same selection could be useful in the opposite direction, as many economic occupations, especially in our time of automatic machines, demand a quick and often rhythmical transition from one activity to another. It is evident that those whose natural dispositions make every mental excitement a preparation not for the identical but for the contrasting stimulation will be naturally equipped for this kind of economic tasks.

XVII

ATTENTION AND FATIGUE

THE problem of monotony may lead us on to other conditions through which attention is hindered and the product of labor thereby decreased. The psychologist naturally first thinks of external distractions of attention. If he turns to practical studies of the actual economic life, he is often decidedly surprised to find how little regard is given to this psychophysical factor. In industrial establishments in which the smallest disturbance in the machine is at once remedied by a mechanic in order that the greatest possible economic effect may be secured, frequently nobody takes any interest in the most destructive disturbances which unnecessarily occur in the subtlest part of the factory mechanism, namely, the attention apparatus of the laborers. Such an interference with attention must, for instance, be recognized when the workingman, instead of devoting himself to one complex function, has to carry out secondary movements which appear to be quite easily performed and not to hinder him in his chief task. Often his own feeling may endorse this impression. Of course the individual differences in this direction are very great. The faculty of carrying on at the same time various independent functions is unequally distributed and the experiment can show this clearly. It is also well known from practical life that some men can easily go on dictating to a stenographer while they are affixing their signature to several hundred circular letters, or can continue their fluent lecture while they are performing experimental demonstrations. With others such a side activity continually interrupts the chief function. Then some succeed better than others in securing a certain automatism of the accessory function to such a point that its special acts do not come to consciousness at all. For example, I watched a laborer who was constantly engaged in a complicated technical performance, and he seemed to give to it his full attention. Nevertheless he succeeded in moving a lever on an automatic machine which stood near by whenever a certain wheel had made fifty revolutions. During all his work he kept counting the revolutions without being conscious of any idea of number. A system of motor reactions had become organized which remained below the threshold of consciousness and which produced only at the fiftieth recurrence the conscious psychical impulse to perform the lever movement. Yet whether the talent for such simultaneous mastery of independent functions be greater or smaller and the demand more or less complex, in every case the principal action must be hampered by the side issue. To be sure, it may sometimes be economically more profitable to allow the hindrance to the chief work in order to save the expense of an extra man to do the side work. In most cases, however, such a consideration is not involved; it is simply an ignoring of the psychological situation. As the accessory work seems easy, its hindering influence on other functions is practically overlooked. Psychological laboratory experiments have shown in many different directions that simultaneous independent activities always disturb and inhibit one another.

We must not forget that even the conversations of the laborers belong in this psychophysical class. Where a continuous strain of attention has produced a state of fatigue, a short conversation will bring a certain relief and relaxation, and the words which the speaker hears in reply will produce a general stimulation of psychical energy for the moment. Moreover, the mere existence of the social conversational intercourse will raise the general emotional mood, and this feeling of social pleasure may be the source from which may spring new psychophysical powers. Nevertheless the fundamental fact, after all, is that any talking during the labor, so far as it is not necessary for the work itself, surely involves a distraction of attention. Here, too, the individual is not conscious of the effect. He feels certain that he can perform his task just as well, and even the pieceworker, who is anxious to earn as much as possible, is convinced that he does not retard himself by conversation. But the experiments which have been carried on in establishments with scientific management speak decidedly against such a supposition. A tyrannical demand for silence would, of course, be felt as cruelty, and no suggestion of a jail-like discipline would be wise in the case of industrial labor, for evident psychological reasons. But various factories in rearranging their establishments according to the principles of scientific management have changed the positions of the workmen so that conversations become more difficult or impossible. The result reported seems to be everywhere a significant increase of production. The individual concentrates his mind on the task with an intensity which seems beyond his reach as long as the inner attitude is adjusted to social contact. The help which is rendered by the feeling of social coöperation, on the other hand, is not removed by the mere abstaining from speaking. Interesting psychopedagogical experiments have, indeed, demonstrated that working in a common room produces better results than isolated activity. This is not true of the most brilliant, somewhat nervous school children, who achieve in their own room at home more than in the classroom. But for the average, which almost alone is in question for life in the factory, the consciousness of common effort is a source of psychophysical reinforcement. This evidently remains effective when the workingmen can see one another, even if the arrangement of the seats precludes the possibility of chatting during the work.

However, by far the more important cause of distraction of attention lies in those disturbances which come from without. Here again the chief interest ought to be attached to those interferences which the workman himself no longer feels as such. In a great printing-shop a woman who was occupied with work which demanded her fullest attention was seated at her task in an aisle where trucking was done. Removing this operator to a quiet corner caused an increase of 25 per cent in her work.[40] To be sure there are many such disturbances in factory life which can hardly be eliminated with the technical means of to-day. For instance, the noise of the machines, which in many factories makes it impossible to communicate except by shouting, must be classed among the real psychological interferences in spite of the fact that the laborers themselves usually feel convinced that they no longer notice it at all. Still more disturbing are strong rhythmical sounds, such as heavy hammer blows which dominate the continuous noises, as they force on every individual consciousness a psychophysical rhythm of reaction which may stand in strong contrast to that of a man's own work. From the incessant inner struggle of the two rhythms, the one suggested by the labor, the other by the external intrusion, quick exhaustion becomes unavoidable.

If it were our purpose to elaborate a real system of psychological economics, we should have to proceed here to a careful study of the influences of fatigue on the industrial achievement. We should have to discuss the various kinds of fatigue and exhaustion, the conditions of restoration, and the whole group of related problems of psychophysics. But this is the one field which has been thoroughly ploughed over by science and by practical life in the course of the last decades. No new suggestion and no new hint of the importance of the problem is needed here. Our short discussion was planned to be confined to those regions which have not been worked up in systematic investigations and for which new devices seemed desirable. Hence we do not reproduce here the rich material of facts which the physiologists and psychophysicists have brought together in the last half-century, the importance of which for industrial labor is perfectly evident. Moreover, the practical applications and the insight into the social needs have transformed the factories themselves into one big laboratory in which the problem of fatigue has been studied by practical experiments. The problem of the dependence of fatigue and output upon the length of the working day has been tested in numberless places with the methods of really exact research, as it was easy to find out how the achievement of the laborers became quantitatively and qualitatively changed by the shortening of the working hours.

When in one civilized country after another the exhaustingly long working days of the industrial wage-earner were shortened more and more, the theoretical discussions of the legislators and of the social reformers were soon supplemented by careful statistical inquiries in the factories. It was found that everywhere, even abstracting from all other cultural and social interests, a moderate shortening of the working day did not involve loss, but brought a direct gain. The German pioneer in the movement for the shortening of the workingman's day, Ernst Abbé, the head of one of the greatest German factories, wrote many years ago that the shortening from nine to eight hours, that is, a cutting-down of more than 10 per cent, did not involve a reduction of the day's product, but an increase, and that this increase did not result from any supplementary efforts by which the intensity of the work would be reinforced in an unhygienic way.[41] This conviction of Abbé still seems to hold true after millions of experiments over the whole globe. But the problem of fatigue has forced itself on the consideration of the men of affairs from still another side. It has been well known for a long while how intimate the relations are between fatigue and industrial accidents. The statistics of the various countries and of the various industries do not harmonize exactly, but a close connection between the number of accidents and the hours of the day can be recognized everywhere. Usually the greatest number of injuries occurs between ten and eleven o'clock in the forenoon and between three and four o'clock in the afternoon. The different distribution of the working hours, and of the pauses for the meals, make the various statistical tables somewhat incomparable. But it can be traced everywhere that in the first working hours in which fatigue does not play any considerable rôle, the number of accidents is small, and that this number sinks again after the long pauses. It is true that the number also becomes somewhat smaller at the end of the forenoon and of the afternoon period, but this seems to have its cause in the fact that with growing fatigue and with the feeling that the end of the working period is near, the rhythm of the activity becomes much slower, and with such slower movements the danger of accidents is greatly reduced. In a similar way the factories have had to give the fullest attention to the fatigue problem in its relation to the distribution of pauses, and above all in its relation to the advisable speed of the machines, the limits of which are set by the fatigue of the workingmen, and still more of the working-women.

The legislatures, the labor unions, and the manufacturers have then had this problem of fatigue constantly before their eyes.[42] On the other hand, the psychologists and physiologists have continuously studied the fatigue and restoration of the muscle system and of the central nervous system, and have analyzed the facts with the subtlest methods. Yet, in spite of this, it cannot be denied that a real mutual enrichment has so far hardly been in question. On the contrary, the whole situation has again demonstrated the old experience. The mere trying and trying again in practical life can never reach the maximum effects which may be secured by systematic, scientifically conducted efforts. On the other side the studies of the theoretical scholars can never yield the highest values for civilization if the problems which offer themselves in practical life are ignored. The theorists have to prepare the ground, and in this preparatory work they must, indeed, remain utterly regardless of any practical situations. But after that a second stage must be reached at which on the foundation of this neutral research special theoretical investigations are undertaken which originate from practical conditions. As long as industrial managers have no contact with the experiments of the laboratory and the experimentalists are shy of any contact with the industrial reality, humanity will pass through social suffering. The hope of mankind will be realized by the mutual fertilization of knowing and doing.

The practical efforts of the factories have, indeed, not yet reached the point at which the greatest possible achievement which can be reached without over-fatigue may be secured. We called the abbreviation of the working day an experimental scheme. The question of reducing the working hours is so simple that no further special experiments are needed. But when we come to the questions of the pauses at work, the speed of work and similar factors related to fatigue, the situation is by far more complicated, and the often capricious changes in the plant have very little in common with a systematic experiment. Some well-known studies of the efficiency engineers clearly demonstrate the possibility of such systematic efforts. The best-known case is probably Taylor's study of the pig-iron handlers of the Bethlehem Steel Company. He found that the gang of 75 men was loading on the average about $12\frac{1}{2}$ tons per man per day. When he discussed with various managers the question of what output would be the possible maximum, they agreed that under premium work, piecework, or any of the ordinary plans for stimulating the men, an output of 18 to 25 tons would be the extreme possibility. Then he proceeded to a systematic study of the fatigue in its relation to the burden and of the best possible relation between working time and resting time. His first efforts to find formulas were unsuccessful, because he calculated only the actual mechanical energy exerted and found that some men were tired after exerting energy of $\frac{1}{8}$ hp., while others seemed to be able to produce the energy of $\frac{1}{2}$ hp. without greater fatigue. But soon he discovered the mistake in his figures.

He had considered only the actual movements, and had neglected the period in which the laborer was not moving and was not exerting energy, but in which a weight was pulling his arms and demanding a corresponding muscular effort. As soon as this muscular achievement was taken into account, too, he found that for each particular weight a definite relation exists between the time that a man is under a heavy load and the time of rest. For the usual loads of 90 pounds, he found that a first-class laborer must not work more than 43 per cent of the working day and must be entirely without load 57 per cent. If the load becomes lighter, the relation is changed. If the workman is handling a half pig weighing 46 pounds, he can be under load 58 per cent of the day and only has to rest during 42 per cent.[43]

As soon as these figures were experimentally secured, Taylor selected fit men, and did not allow them to lift and to carry the loads as they pleased, but every movement was exactly prescribed by foremen who timed exactly the periods of work and rest. If he had simply promised his men a high premium in case they should carry more than the usual 12 tons a day, they would have burdened themselves as heavily as possible and would have carried the load as quickly as possible, thus completely exhausting themselves after three or four hours of labor. In spite of such senseless exaggeration of effort in the first hours, the total output for the day would have been relatively small. Now the foremen determined exactly when every individual should lift and move the load and when he should sit quietly. The result was that the men, without greater fatigue, were able to carry $47\frac{1}{2}$ tons a day instead of the $12\frac{1}{2}$ tons. Their wages were increased 60 per cent. Such a trivial illustration demonstrates very clearly the extreme difference between an increase of the economic achievement by scientific, experimental investigation and a mere enforcing of more work by artificially whipping-up the mind with promises of extraordinary wages. Yet even such rules as the scientific management engineers have formed, may be elaborated to more lasting prescriptions as soon as the purely psychological factors are brought more into the foreground and are approached with the careful analysis of the experimental psychologist.

Such a systematic psychological inquiry is the more important for questions of fatigue, as we know that the subjective feeling of displeasure in fatigue is no reliable measure for the objective fatigue, that is, for the real reduction of the ability for work. Daily experience teaches us how easily some people overstep the limits of normal fatigue, and in extreme cases even come to a nervous breakdown because nature did not protect them by the timely appearance of strong fatigue feelings. On the other hand, we find many men and still more women who feel tired even after a small exertion, because they did not learn early to inhibit the superficial feelings of fatigue, or because the sensations of fatigue have in fact a certain abnormal intensity in their case. The question how far the psychophysical apparatus has really been exhausted by a certain effort must be answered with the help of objective research and not on the basis of mere subjective feelings. But such objective measurements demand systematic experiments in the laboratory.

The experiments which really have been carried on in the laboratory as yet, as far as they were not merely physiological, have on the whole been confined to so-called mental labor, and were essentially devoted to problems of school instruction or medical diagnosis. We have no doubt excellent experiments which are devoted to the study of the individual differences of exhaustion, fatigue, exhaustibility, ability to recover the lost energy, ability to learn from practice, and so on, but they are still exclusively adjusted to the needs of the school-teacher and of the nerve specialist and would hardly be immediately useful to the

THE BEST POSSIBLE WORK

manager of a factory. We shall need a long careful series of investigations in order to determine
how far those manifold results from experiments
with memory work, thought work, writing work,
and so on can be applied to the work which the
industrial laborer is expected to perform.

XVIII

PHYSICAL AND SOCIAL INFLUENCES ON THE WORKING POWER

THE increase and decrease of the ability to do good work depends of course not only upon the direct fatigue from labor and the pauses for rest; a large variety of other factors may lead to fluctuations which are economically important. The various hours of the day, the seasons of the year, the atmospheric conditions of weather and climate, may have such influence. Some elements of this interplay have been cleared up in recent years. Just as the experiments of pedagogical psychology have determined the exact curve of efficiency during the period of an hour in school, so other investigations have traced the typical curve of psychical efficiency throughout the day and the year. Sociological and criminological statistics concerning the fluctuations in the behavior of the masses, common-sense experience of practical life, and finally, economic statistics concerning the quantity and quality of industrial output in various parts of the day and of the year, have supplemented one another. The systematic assistance of the psychological laboratory, however, has been confined to the educational aspect of the problem. Psychological experiments have determined how the achievement of the youth in the schoolroom changes with the months of the year and the hours of the day. It seems as if it could not be difficult to secure here, too, a connection between exact experiment and economic work. Much will have to be reduced to individual variations. The laboratory has already confirmed the experience of daily life that there are morning workers whose strongest psychophysical efficiency comes immediately after the night's rest, while the day's work fatigues them more and more; and that there are evening workers who in the morning still remain under the after effects of the night's sleep, and who slowly become fresher and fresher from the stimuli of the day. It would seem not impossible to undertake a systematic selection of various individuals under this point of view, as different industrial tasks demand a different distribution of efficiency between morning and night.

Such a selection and adjustment may be economically still more important with reference to the fluctuations during the course of the year. Economic inquiries, for instance, have suggested that younger and older workingmen who ordinarily show the same efficiency become unequal in their ability to do good work in the spring months, and the economists have connected this inequality with sexual conditions. But other factors as well, especially the blood circulation of the organism and the resulting reactions to external temperature, different gland activities, and so on, cause great personal differences in efficiency during the various seasons of the year. Inasmuch as we know many economic occupations in which the chief demand is made in one or another period of the year, a systematic study of these individual variations might be of high economic value, where large numbers are involved, and might contribute much to the individual comfort of the workers. But a constant relation to day and year also seems to exist independent of all personal variations. When the sun stands at its meridian, a minimum of efficiency is to be expected and a similar minimum is to be found at the height of summer. Correspondingly we have an increase of the total psychical efficiency in winter-time. During the spring-time the behavior seems, as far as the investigations go, to be different in the intellectual and in the psychomotor activities. It is claimed that the efficiency of the intellectual functions decreases as the winter recedes, but that the efficiency of psychomotor impulses increases.[44]

THE BEST POSSIBLE WORK

The influences of the daily temperature, of the weather and of the seasons may be classed among the physical conditions of efficiency. We may group with them the effects of nourishment, of stimulants, of sleep, and so on. As far as the relations between these external factors and purely bodily muscle work are involved, the interests of the psychologists are not engaged. But it is evident that every one of these relations also has its psychological aspect, and that a really scientific psychotechnical treatment of these problems can become possible only through the agency of psychological experiments. We have excellent experimental investigations concerning the influence of the loss of sleep on intellectual labor and on simple psychomotor activities. But it would be rather arbitrary to deduce from the results of those researches anything as to the effect of reduction of sleep on special economic occupations. Yet such knowledge would be of high importance. We have in the literature concerned with accidents in transportation numerous popular discussions about the destructive influence of loss of sleep on the attention of the locomotive engineer or of the helmsman or of the chauffeur, but an analysis of the particular psychophysical processes does not as yet exist and can be expected only from systematic experiments. Nor has the influence of hunger on psychotechnical activities been studied in a satisfactory way.

A number of psychological investigations have been devoted to the study of the influence of alcohol on various psychical functions and in this field at least the strictly economic problem of industrial labor has sometimes been touched. We have the much quoted and much misinterpreted experiments [45] which were carried on in Germany with typesetters. The workmen received definite quantities of heavy wine at a particular point in the work and the number of letters which they were able to set during the following quarter-hours were measured and compared with their normal achievement in fifteen minutes. The reduction of efficiency amounted on the average to 15 per cent of the output. It may be mentioned that the loss referred only to the quantity of the work and not at all to the quality. The well-known subjective illusory feeling of the subjects was not lacking; they themselves believed that the wine had reinforced their working power. As soon as such experiments are put into the service of economic life, they will have to be carried on with much more accurate adjustment to the special conditions, with subtler gradation of the stimuli, and especially with careful study of individual factors. But at first it seems more in the interest of the practical task that the extremely complicated problem of the influence of alcohol be followed up by purely theoretical research in the laboratory in order that the effect may be resolved into its various components. We must first find the exact facts concerning the influence of alcohol on elementary processes of mental life, such as perception, attention, memory, and so on, and this will slowly prepare the way for the complete economic experiment.

At present the greatest significance for the economic field may be attached to those alcohol experiments which dealt with the apprehension of the outer world. They proved a reduction in the ability to grasp the impressions and a narrowing of the span of consciousness. The indubitable decrease of certain memory powers, of the acuity in measuring distance, of the time estimation, and similar psychical disturbances after alcohol, must evidently be of high importance for industry and transportation, while the well-known increase of the purely sensory sensibility, especially of the visual acuity after small doses of alcohol, hardly plays an important rôle in practical life. The best-known and experimentally most studied effect of alcohol, the increase of motor excitability, also evidently has its importance for industrial achievements. It cannot be denied that this facility of the motor impulses after small doses of alcohol is not a real gain, which might be utilized economically, but is ultimately an injury to the apparatus, even if we abstract from the retardation of the reaction which comes as an after-effect. The alcoholic facilitation, after all, reduces the certainty and the perfection of the reaction and creates conditions under which wrong, and this in economic life means often dangerous, motor responses arise. The energy of the motor discharge suffers throughout from the alcohol.

Some experiments which were recently carried on with reference to the influence of alcohol on the power of will seem to have especial significance for the field of economic activity. The method applied in the experiment was the artificial creation of an exactly measurable resistance to the will-impulse directed toward a purpose. The experiment had to determine what power of resistance could be overcome by the will and how far this energy changes under the influence of alcohol. For this end combinations of meaningless syllables were learned and repeated until they formed a close connection in memory. If one syllable was given, the mechanical tendency of the mind was to reproduce the next syllable in the memorized series. The will-intention was then directed toward breaking this memory type. For instance, it was demanded, when a syllable was called, that the subject should not answer with the next following syllable, but with a rhyming syllable. This will-impulse easily succeeded when the syllables to be learned had been repeated only a few times, while after a very frequent repetition the memory connection offered a resistance which the simple will-intention could not break. The syllable which followed in the series rushed to the mind before the intention to seek a rhyming syllable could be realized. The number of repetitions thus became a measure for the power of the will. After carrying out these experiments at first under normal conditions, they were repeated while the subjects were under the influence of exactly graded doses of alcohol.[46] From such simple tasks the experiment was turned to more and more complex ones of similar structure. All together they showed clearly that the alcohol did not influence the ability to make the will effective and that the actual decrease of achievement results from a decrease in the ability to grasp the material. As long as the alcohol doses are small, this feeling of decreased ability stirs up a reinforcement in the tension of the will-impulse. This may go to such an extent that the increased will-effort not only compensates for the reduced understanding, but even over-compensates for it, producing an improvement in the mental work. But as soon as the alcohol doses amount to about 100 cubic centimeters, the increased tension of the will is no longer sufficient to balance the paralyzing effect in the understanding. Yet it must not be overlooked that in all these experiments only isolated will acts were in question which were separated from one another by pauses of rest. Evidently, however, the technical laborer is more often in a situation in which not isolated impulses, but a continuous tension of the will is demanded. How far such an uninterrupted will-function is affected by alcohol has not as yet been studied with the exact means of the experiment.

To be sure an obvious suggestion would be that the whole problem, as far as economics, and especially industry, are concerned, might be solved in a simpler way than by the performance of special psychological experiments, namely, by the complete elimination of alcohol itself from the life of the wage-earner. The laboratory experiment which seems to demonstrate a reduction of objective achievement in the case of every important mental function merely supplements in exact language the appalling results indicated by criminal statistics, disease statistics, and inheritance statistics. It seems as if the time had come when scientists could not with a good conscience suggest any other remedy than the merciless suppression of alcohol. Indeed, there can be no doubt that alcohol is one of the worst enemies of civilized life, and it is therefore almost with regret that the scientist must acknowledge that all the psychological investigations, which have so often been misused in the partisan writings of prohibitionists, are not a sufficient basis to justify the demand for complete abstinence.

First, newer experiments make it very clear that many of the so-called effects of alcohol which the experiment has demonstrated are produced or at least heightened by influences of suggestion. Experiments which have been carried on in England for the study of that point show clearly that certain psychical disturbances which seem to result from small doses of alcohol fail to appear as soon as the subject does not know that he has taken alcohol. For that purpose it was necessary to eliminate the odor, and this was accomplished by introducing the beverages into the organism by a stomach pump. When by this method sometimes water and sometimes diluted alcohol was given without the knowledge of the subject, the usual effects of small doses of alcohol did not arise. But another point is far more important. We may take it for granted that alcohol reduces the ability for achievement as soon as such very small doses are exceeded. But from the standpoint of economic life we have no right to consider a reduction of the psychical ability to produce work as identical with a decrease in the economic value of the personality. Such a view would be right if the influence necessarily set in at the beginning of the working period. But if, for instance, a moderate quantity of beer is introduced into the organism after the closing of the working day, it would certainly produce an artificial reduction of the psychical ability, and yet this decrease of psychophysical activity might be advantageous to the total economic achievement of the workingman in the course of the week or the year. To be sure the glass of beer in the evening paralyzes certain inhibitory centres of the brain and therefore puts the mind out of gear, but such a way of expressing it may easily be misleading, as it suggests too much that a real injury is done. From the point of view of scientific psychology, we must acknowledge that such a paralyzing effect in certain parts of the psychophysical system sets in with every act of attention and reaches its climax in sleep, which surely does no harm to the mind. It may be thoroughly advantageous for the total work of the normal, healthy, average workingman if the after effects of the motor excitement of the day are eliminated by a mild, short alcoholic poi-

231

soning in the evening. It may produce that narrowing and dulling of consciousness which extinguishes the cares and sorrows of the day and secures the night's sleep, and through it increased efficiency the next morning. Systematic experiments with exact relation to the various technical demands must slowly bring real insight into this complex situation. The usual hasty generalization from a few experiments with alcohol for partisan interests is surely not justified in the present unsatisfactory state of knowledge.[47]

Perhaps we know still less of the influences which coffee, tea, tobacco, sweets, and so on exert on the life of the industrial worker. It will be wise to resolve these stimuli in daily use into their elements and to study the effects of each element in isolated form. To know, for instance, the effects of caffein on the psychophysical activities does not mean to know the effects of tea or coffee, which contain a variety of other substances besides the caffein, substances which may be supposed to modify the effect of the caffein. Yet the first step must in this case be the study of the effects of the isolated caffein, before the total influences of the familiar beverages can be followed up. An excellent investigation of this caffein effect on various psychological and psychomotor functions has recently been completed.[48] When the caffein effect on tapping movements was studied, it was found that it works as a stimulation, sometimes preceded by a slight initial retardation. It persists from one to two hours after doses of from one to three grains and as long as four hours after doses of six grains. The steadiness test showed a slight nervousness after several hours after doses of from one to four grains. After six grains there is pronounced unsteadiness. A complex test in coördination indicated that the effect of small amounts of caffein is a stimulation and that of large amounts a retardation. Correspondingly the speed of performance in typewriting is heightened by small doses of caffein and retarded by larger doses. In both cases the quality of the performance as measured by the number of errors is superior to the normal result.

The influences of the physiological stimulants have many points of contact with the effects of social entertainment, the significance of which for the economic life is still rather unknown in any exact detail. Many factories in which the labor is noiseless, as in the making of cigars, have introduced gramophone music or reading aloud, and it is easy to understand theoretically that a certain animating effect results, which stimulates the whole psychophysical activity. But only the experiment would be able to decide how this stimulation is related, for instance, to the distraction of attention, which is necessarily involved, or how it influences various periods of the work and various types of work, how far it is true that the musical key exerts an exciting or relaxing influence, what intensity and what local position, what rhythm and what duration of such æsthetic stimuli, would bring the best possible economic results. We all have read of the favorable effects which were secured in a factory when a cat was brought into every working-room in which women laborers were engaged in especially fatiguing work. The cat became a living toy for the employees, which stimulated their social consciousness. In not a few plants the reinforced achievement is explained by the social means of entertainment which have been introduced under the pressure of modern philanthropic ideas. The lounging-rooms with the newspapers and periodicals, the clubrooms with libraries, the excursions and dances and patriotic festivities, fill up the reservoir of psychophysical energies. As a matter of course all the social movements which enhance the consciousness of solidarity among the laborers and the feeling of security as to their future development in their career have a similar effect of reinforcing the normal psychical achievement.

As the strongest factor, finally, the direct material interest must be added to these conditions. The literature of political economy is full of discussions of the effect of increase of wages, of the payment of bonuses and premiums, of piece-wages, of promised pensions, and, as far as Europe is concerned, of state insurance. In short, the whole individual financial situation in its relation to the psychophysical achievement of the wage-earner is a favorite topic of economic inquiry. We cannot participate here in these inexhaustible discussions, because all these questions are to-day still so endlessly far from the field of psychological experiments. Nevertheless we ought not to forget the experience through which general experimental psychology has gone in the last few decades. When the first experiments were undertaken in order to deal systematically with the mental life, the friends of this new science and its opponents agreed, on the whole, in the belief that certainly only the most elementary phenomena of consciousness, the sensations and the reactions of impulses, would be accessible to the new method. The opponents naturally compared this modest field with the great problems of the mental totality, and therefore ridiculed the new narrow task as unimportant. The friends, on the other hand, were eager to follow the fresh path, because they were content to gain real exactitude by the experiment at least in these simplest questions. Yet as soon as the new independent workshops were established for the young science, it was discovered that the method was able to open fields in which no one had anticipated its usefulness. The experiments turned to the problems of attention, of memory, of imagination, of feeling, of judgment, of character, of æsthetic experience and so on. It is not improbable that the method of the economic psychological experiment may also quickly lead beyond the more elementary problems, as soon as it is systematically applied, and then it, too, may conquer regions of inquiry in which to-day no exact calculation of the psychological factors seems possible.

If such an advance is to be a steady one, the economic psychologist will emancipate himself from the chance question of what problems are at this moment important for commerce and industry and will proceed systematically step by step from those results which the psychological laboratory has yielded under the non-economic points of view. Many previous psychological or psychophysical inquiries almost touch the problems of industrial achievement. For instance, the experiments on imitation, which psychophysicists have carried on in purely theoretical or pedagogical interests, move parallel to industrial experiences. It is well known that the pacemaker plays his rôle not only in the field of sport but also in the factory. The rhythm of one laborer gains controlling importance for the others, who instinctively imitate him. Some plants even have automatically working machines with the special intention that the sharp rhythm of these lifeless forerunners shall produce an involuntary imitation in the psychophysical system. In a similar way many laboratory investigations on suggestion and suggestibility point to such economic processes, and it seems to me that especially the studies on the influence of the ideas of purpose which are being undertaken nowadays in many psychological laboratories may easily be connected with the problems of economic life. We know how the consciousness of the task to be performed has an organizing influence on the system of those psychophysical acts which lead to the goal. The experiment has shown under which conditions this effect can be reinforced and under which reduced. Pedagogical experiments have also shown exactly what influence belongs to the consciousness of the approach to the end of work; the feeling of the nearness of the close heightens the achievement, even of the fatigued subject. It would not be difficult to connect psychophysical experiments of this kind with the problems of the task and bonus system, which is nowadays so much discussed in industrial life. The practical successes seem to prove that the individual can do more with equal effort if he does not stand before an unlimited mass of work of which he has to do as much as possible in the course of the day, but if he is before a definitely determined, limited task with the demand that he complete it in an exactly calculated time. Scientific management has made far-reaching use of this principle, but whether constant results for the various industries can be hoped for from such methods must again be ascertained by the psychological experiment.

These hopes surely will not weaken the interest of the psychologist for those many psychological methods which lie outside of the experimental research. A sociologist, who himself had been a laborer in his earlier life, undertook in Germany last year an inquiry into the psychological status of the laborers' achievement by the questionnaire method.[49] He sent to 8000 workingmen in the mining industries, textile industries, and metal industries, blanks containing 26 questions, and received more than 5000 replies. The questions referred to the pleasure and interest in the work, to preferences, to fatigue, to the thoughts during the work, to the means of recreation, to the attitude toward the wages, to the emotional situation, and so on. The 5000 answers allowed manifold classifications. The various mental types of men could be examined, the influence of the machine, the attitude toward monotony, the changes of pleasure and interest in the work with the age of the laborer, the time at which fatigue becomes noticeable, and so on. Many psychological elements of industrial life thus come to a sharp focus and the strong individual differences could not be brought out in a more characteristic way. Yet, all taken together, even such a careful investigation on a psychostatistical basis strongly suggests that a few careful experimental investigations could lead further than such a heaping-up of material gathered from men who are untrained in self-observation and in accurate reports, and above all who are accessible to any kind of suggestion and preconceived idea. The experimental method is certainly not the only one which can contribute to reforms in industrial life and the reinforcement of industrial efficiency, but all signs indicate that the future will find it the most productive and most reliable.

PART III

THE BEST POSSIBLE EFFECT

PART III

THE BEST POSSIBLE EFFECT

XIX

THE SATISFACTION OF ECONOMIC DEMANDS

EVERY economic function comes in contact with the mental life of man, first from the fact that the work is produced by the psyche of personalities. This gave us the material for the first two parts of our discussion. We asked what mind is best fitted for the particular kind of work, and how the mind can be led to the best output of work. But it is evident that the real meaning of the economic process expresses itself in an entirely different contact between work and mind. The economic activity is separated from all other processes in the world, not by the fact that it involves labor and achievement by personalities, but by the fact that this labor satisfies a certain group of human desires which we acknowledge as economic. The mere performance of labor, with all the psychical traits of attention and fatigue and will-impulses and personal qualities, does not in itself constitute anything of economic value.

For instance, the sportsman who climbs a glacier also performs such a fatiguing activity which demands the greatest effort of attention and will; and yet the psychotechnics of sport do not belong in economic psychology, because this mountain climbing does not satisfy economic desires. The ultimate characteristic which designates an activity as economic is accordingly a certain effect on human souls. The whole whirl of the economic world is ultimately controlled by the purpose of satisfying certain psychical desires. Hence this psychical effect is still more fundamental for the economic process than its psychical origin in the mental conditions of the worker. The task of psychotechnics is accordingly to determine by exact psychological experiments how this mental effect, the satisfaction of economic desires, can be secured in the quickest, in the easiest, in the safest, in the most enduring, and in the most satisfactory way.

But we must not deceive ourselves as to the humiliating truth that so far not the slightest effort has been made toward the answering of this central scientific question. If the inquiry into the psychical effects were really to be confined to this problem of the ultimate satisfaction of economic desires, scientific psychology could not contribute any results and could not offer anything but hopes and wishes for the future. At the first glance it might appear as if just here a large amount of literature exists; moreover, a literature rich in excellent investigations and ample empirical material. On the one side the political economists, with their theories of economic value and their investigations concerning the conditions of prices and the development of luxury, the calculation of economic values from pleasure and displeasure and many similar studies, have connected the economic processes with mental life; on the other side the philosophers, with their theories of value, have not confined themselves to the ethical and æsthetic motives, but have gone deeply into the economic life too. While such studies of the economists and of the philosophers are chiefly meant to serve theoretical understanding, it might seem easy to deduce from them technical practical prescriptions as well. If we know that under particular conditions certain demands will be satisfied, we draw the conclusion that we must realize those conditions whenever such demands are to be satisfied. The theoretical views of the economists and of the philosophers of value might thus be directly translated into psychotechnical advice.

As soon as we look deeper into the situation, we must recognize that this surface impression is entirely misleading. Certainly whenever the philosophers or political economists discuss the problems of value and of the satisfaction of human demands, they are using psychological terms, but the whole meaning which they attach to these terms, feeling, emotion, will, desire, pleasure, displeasure, joy, and pain, is essentially different from that which controls the causal explanations of scientific psychology. We cannot enter into the real fundamental questions here, which are too often carelessly ignored even in scientific quarters. Too often psychology is treated, even by psychologists, as if it covered every possible systematic treatment of inner experience, and correspondingly outsiders like the economists fancy that they are on psychological ground and are handling psychological conceptions as soon as they make any statements concerning the inner life. But if we examine the real purposes and presuppositions of the various sciences, we must recognize that the human experience can be looked on from two entirely different points of view. Only from one of the two does it present itself as psychological material and as a fit object for psychological study. From the other point of view, which is no less valuable and no less important for the understanding of our inner life, human experience offers itself as a reality with which psychology as such has nothing to do, even though it may be difficult to eliminate the usual psychological words.

The psychologist considers human experience as a series of objects for consciousness. All the perceptions and memory ideas and imaginative ideas and feelings and emotions, are taken by him as mental objects of which consciousness becomes aware, and his task is to describe and to explain them and to find the laws for their succession. He studies them as a naturalist studies the chemical elements or the stars. It makes no difference whether his explanation leads him to connect these mental contents with brain processes as one theory proposes, or with subconscious processes as another theory suggests. The entirely different aspect of inner life is the one which is most natural in our ordinary intercourse. Whenever we give an account of our inner life or are interested in the experience of our friends, we do not consider how their mental experiences as such objective contents of consciousness are to be described and explained, but we take them as inner actions and attitudes toward the world, and our aim is not to describe and to explain them but to interpret and to understand them. We do not seek their elements but their meaning, we do not seek their causes and effects but their inner relations and their inner purposes. In short, we do not take them at all as objects but as functions of the subject, and our dealing with them has no similarity to the method of the naturalist.

This method of practical life in which we seek to express and to understand a meaning, and relate every will-act to its aim, is not confined to the mere popular aspect; it can lead to very systematic scholarly treatment. It is exactly the treatment which is fundamental in the case of all history, for example, or of law, or of logic. That is, the historian makes us understand the meaning of a personality of the past and is really interested in past events only as far as human needs are to be interpreted. It would be pseudo-psychology, if we called such an account in the truly historical spirit a psychological description and explanation. The student of law interprets the meaning of the will of the legislator; he does not deal with the idea of the law as a psychological content. And the logician has nothing to do with the idea as a conscious object in the mind; he asks as to the inner relations of it and as to the conclusions from the premises. In short, wherever historical interpretations or logical deductions are needed, we move on in the sphere of human life as it presents itself from the standpoint of immediate true experience without artificially moulding it into the conceptions of psychology. On the other hand, as soon as the psychological method is applied, this immediate life meaning of human experience is abandoned, and instead of it is gained the possibility of considering the whole experience as a system of causes and effects. Mental life is then no longer what it is to us in our daily intercourse, because it is reconstructed for the purposes of this special treatment, just as the water which we drink is no longer our beverage if we consider it under the point of view of chemistry as a combination of hydrogen and oxygen. Hence we have not two statements one of which is true and the other ultimately untrue; on the contrary, both are true. We have a perfect right to give the value of truth to our experience with water as a refreshing drink, and also to the formula of the chemist. With a still better right we may claim that both kinds of mental experience are equally true. Hence not a word of objection is raised against the discussions of the historians and the philosophers, if we insist that their so-called psychology stands outside of the really descriptive and explanatory account of mental life, and is therefore not psychology in the technical sense of the word.

It is this historical attitude which controls all the studies of the political economists. They

speak of the will-acts of the individuals and of
their demands and desires and satisfactions, but
they do not describe and explain them; they want
to interpret and understand them. They may
analyze the motives of the laborer or of the manufacturer, but those motives and impulses interest
them not as contents of consciousness, but only
as acts which are directed toward a goal. The aim
toward which these point by their meaning, and
not the elements from which they are made up
or their causes and effects, is the substance of
such economic studies. For such a subjective
account of the meaning of actions the only problem is, indeed, the correct understanding and interpretation, and the consistent psychologist who
knows that it is not his task to interpret but to
explain has no right to raise any questions here.
It is, therefore, only a confusing disturbance, if
a really psychological, causal explanation is mixed
into the interpretation of such a system of will-
acts and purposes. It is true we find this confusion
in many modern works on economics. Economists know that a scientific explanatory study of
the human mind exists, and they have a vague
feeling that they have no right to ignore this real
psychology, instead of recognizing that the psychology really has nothing to do with their particular problem. The result is that they constantly

try to discuss the impulses and instincts, the hunger and thirst and sexual desire, and the higher demands for fighting and playing and acquiring, for seeking power and social influence, as a psychologist would discuss them, referring them to biological and physiological conditions and explaining them causally. Yet as soon as they come to their real problems and enter into the interpretation and meaning of these economic energies, they naturally slide back into the historical, economic point of view and discuss the economic relations of men without any reference to their psychologizing preambles. The application of the psychological, scientific method to the true economic experience is therefore not secured at all in this way. The demands and volitions which they disentangle are not the ones which the psychophysiologist studies, because they are left in their immediate form of life reality. They are accordingly inaccessible to the point of view of experimental psychology, and nothing can be expected from such interpretative discussions of the economists for the psychotechnics at which the psychologist is aiming. Even where the political economists deal with the problems of value in exact language, nothing is gained for the kind of insight for which the psychologist hopes, and the psychologists must therefore go on with their own methods, if they are ever to reach a causal understanding of the means by which a satisfaction of the economic demands may be effected.

So far the psychologists have not even started to examine these economic feelings, demands, and satisfactions with the means of laboratory psychology. Hence no one can say beforehand how it ought to be done and how to gain access to the important problems, inasmuch as the right formulation of the problem and the selection of the right method would here as everywhere be more than half of the solution. It must be left to the development of science for the right starting-point and the right methods to be discovered. Sometimes, to be sure, the experiment has at least approached this group of economic questions. For instance, the investigations of the so-called psychophysical law have often been brought into contact with the experiences of ownership and acquirement. The law, well known to every student of psychology, is that the differences of intensity in two pairs of sensations are felt as equal, when the two pairs of stimuli are standing in the same relation. The difference between the intensities of the light sensations from 10 candles and 11 candles is equal to that from 50 candles and 55 candles, from 100 candles and 110, from 500 candles and 550: that is, the difference of one additional candle between 10 and 11 appears just as great as the difference of 50 candles between 500 and 550. The psychologists have claimed that in a corresponding way the same feeling of difference arises when the amounts of possessions stand in the same relation. That is, the man who owns $100 feels the gain or loss of $1 as much as one who owns $100,000 feels the gain or loss of $1000. Not the absolute amount of the difference, but the relative value of the increase or decrease is the decisive influence on the psychological effect. Some experimental investigations concerning feelings have also come near to the economic boundaries. The study of the contrast feelings and of the relativity of feelings, for instance, has points of contact with the economic problem of how far economic progress, with its stirring up and satisfying of continually new demands, really adds to the quantity of human enjoyment. In other words, how far are those sociologists right who are convinced that by the technical complexity of modern life, with all its comforts and mechanizations, the level of individual life is raised, but that the oscillations about this average level remain the same and produce the same amount of pleasure and pain? The technical advance would therefore bring no increase of human pleasure.

We might also put into this class the meagre

experimental investigations concerning the mutual influence of feelings. When sound, light, and touch impressions, each of which, isolated, produces a feeling of a certain degree, are combined with one another, the experiment can show very characteristic changes in the intensity of pleasure and displeasure. From such routine experiments of the laboratory it might not be difficult to come to more complex experiments on the mutual relations of feeling values and especially of the combinations of pleasure with displeasure. This would lead to an insight into the processes which are involved in the fixing of prices, as they are always dependent upon the pleasure in the acquisition and the displeasure in the outlay. The exact psychology of the future may thus very well determine the conditions under which the best effects for the satisfaction of economic demands may be secured, but our present-day science is still far from such an achievement: and it seems hardly justifiable to propose methods to-day, as it would be like drawing a map with detailed paths for a primeval forest which is still inaccessible.

XX

EXPERIMENTS ON THE EFFECTS OF ADVERTISEMENTS

WE have said that the time has not yet come for discussing from the standpoint of experimental psychology the means to secure the ultimate effects of economic life, namely, the satisfaction of economic demands. If this were the only effect which had economic significance, this whole last part of our little book would have to remain a blank, as we wanted to deal here with the securing of the best effects after having studied the securing of the best man and of the best work. Yet these ultimate ends are certainly not the only mental effects which become important in the course of economic processes. In order to reach that final end of the economic movement, often an unlimited number of part processes distributed over space and time must coöperate. The satisfaction of our thirst in a tea-room may be a trivial illustration of such a final effect, but it is clear that in order to produce this ultimate mental effect of satisfying the thirst, thousands of economic processes must have preceded. To bring the tea and the sugar and the lemon to the table, the porcelain cup and the silver spoon, wage-earners, manufacturers and laborers, exporters, importers, storekeepers, salesmen, and customers had to coöperate. Among such part processes which serve the economic achievement are always many which succeed only if they produce characteristic effects in human minds. The propaganda which the storekeeper makes, for instance, his display and his posters, serve the economic interplay by psychical effects without themselves satisfying any ultimate economic demand. They must attract the passer-by or impress the reader or stimulate his impulse to buy, and through all this they reach an end which is in itself not final, as no human desire to read advertisements exists. When the salesman influences the customer to buy something which may later help to satisfy a real economic demand, the art of his suggestive words secures a mental effect which again is in itself not ultimate. If the manufacturer influences his employees to work with more attention or with greater industry, or if the community stirs up the desire for luxury or the tendency to saving, we have mental effects which are of economic importance without being really ultimate economic effects.

As far as these effects are necessary and justified stages leading to the ultimate satisfaction of economic demands, it certainly is the duty of applied psychology to bring psychological experience and exact methods into their service. We emphasize the necessary and justified character of these steps, as it is evident that psychological methods may be made use of also by those who aim toward mental effects which are unjustified and which are not necessary for the real satisfaction of valuable demands. Psychological laws can also be helpful in fraudulent undertakings or in advertisements for unfair competition. The psychotechnical scientist cannot be blamed if the results of his experiments are misused for immoral purposes, just as the chemist is not responsible if chemical knowledge is aplied to the construction of anarchistic bombs. But while psychology, as we have emphasized before, cannot from its own point of view determine the value of the end, the psychologist as a human being is certainly willing to coöperate only where the soundness and correctness of the ends are evident from the point of view of social welfare.

In order to demonstrate the principle of this kind of psychotechnical help with fuller detail, at least by one illustration, I may discuss the case of the advertisements, the more as this problem has already been taken up in a somewhat systematic way by the psychological laboratories. We have a number of careful experimental investigations referring to the memory-value, the attention-value, the suggestion-value, and other mental effects of the printed business advertisements. Of course this group of experimental investigations at once suggests an objection which we cannot ignore. A business advertisement, as it appears in the newspapers, is such an extremely trivial thing and so completely devoted to the egotistical desire for profit that it seems undignified for the scientist to spend his time on such nothings and to shoot sparrows with his laboratory cannon-balls. But on the one side nothing can be unworthy of thorough study from a strictly theoretical point of view. The dirtiest chemical substance may become of greatest importance for chemistry, and the ugliest insect for zoölogy. On the other side, if the practical point of view of the applied sciences is taken, the importance of the inquiry may stand in direct relation to the intensity of the human demand which is to be satisfied by the new knowledge, Present-day society is so organized that the economic advertisement surely serves a need, and its intensity is expressed by the well-known fact that in every year billions are paid for advertising. Measured by the amount of expenditure, advertising has become one of the largest and economically most important human industries. It is, then, not astonishing that scientists consider it worth while to examine the exact foundations of this industry, but it is surprising that this industry could reach such an enormous development without being guided by the spirit of scientific exactitude which appears a matter of course in every other large business. As it is a function of science to study the physics of incandescent lamps or gas motors so as to bring the economically most satisfactory devices into the service of the community, it cannot be less important from the standpoint of national economics to study scientifically the efficiency of the advertisements in order that the national means may in this industry, too, secure the greatest possible effects. It is only a secondary point that experiments of this kind are of high interest to the theoretical scientist as well. For us the advertisement is simply an instrument constructed to satisfy certain human demands by its effects on the mind. It is a question for psychology to determine the conditions under which this instrument may be best adapted to its purpose.

The mental effect of a well-adapted advertisement is manifold. It appeals to the memory. Whatever we read at the street corner, or in the pages of the newspaper or magazine, is not printed with the idea that we shall immediately turn to the store, but first of all with the expectation that we keep the content of the advertisement in our memory for a later purchase. It will therefore be the more valuable the more vividly it forces itself on the memory. But if practical books about the art of advertising usually presuppose that this influence on the memory will be proportionate to the effect on the attention, the psychologist cannot fully agree. The advertisement may attract the attention of the reader strongly and yet by its whole structure may be unfit to force on the memory its characteristic content, especially the name of the firm and of the article. The pure memory-value is especially important, as according to a well-known psychological law the pleasure in mere recognition readily attaches itself to the recognized object. The customer who has the choice among various makes and brands in the store may not have any idea how far one is superior to another, but the mere fact that one among them bears a name which has repeatedly approached his consciousness before through advertisements is sufficient to arouse a certain warm feeling of acquaintance, and by a transposition of feeling this pleasurable tone accentuates the attractiveness of that make and leads to its selection. This indirect help through the memory-value is economically no less important than the direct service.

THE EFFECTS OF ADVERTISEMENTS

In order to produce a strong effect on memory the advertisement must be easily apprehensible. Psychological laboratory experiments with exact time-measurement of the grasping of various advertisements of the same size for the same article, but in different formulations, demonstrated clearly how much easier or harder the apprehension became through relatively small changes. No mistake in the construction of the advertisement causes so much waste as a grouping which makes the quick apperception difficult. The color, the type, the choice of words, every element, allows an experimental analysis, especially by means of time-measurement. If we determine in thousandths of a second the time needed to recognize the characteristic content of an advertisement, we may discriminate differences which would escape the naïve judgment, and yet which in practical life are of considerable consequence, as the effect of a deficiency is multiplied by the number of readers.

We must insist on the further demand that the advertisement make a vivid impression, so that it may influence the memory through its vividness. Size is naturally the most frequent condition for the increase of vividness, but only the relative size is decisive. The experiment shows that the full-page advertisement in a folio magazine does not influence the memory more than the full page in a quarto magazine, if the reader is for the time adjusted to the particular size. No less important than the size is the originality and the unusual form, the vivid color, the skillful use of empty spaces, the associative elements, the appeal to humor or to curiosity, to sympathy or to antipathy. Every emotion can help to impress the content of the advertisement on the involuntary memory. Unusual announcements concerning the prices or similar factors move in the same direction.

Together with the question of the apprehension and the vividness of the impression, we must acknowledge the frequency of repetition as an equally important factor. We know from daily life how an indifferent advertisement can force itself on our mind, if it appears daily in the same place in the newspaper or is visible on every street corner. But the psychologically decisive factor here is not the fact of the mere repetition of the impression, but rather the stimulation of the attention which results from the repetition. If we remained simply passive and received the impression the second and third and fourth time with the same indifference with which we noticed it the first time, the mere summation would not be sufficient for a strong effect. But the second impression awakes the consciousness of recognition, thus exciting the attention, and through it we now turn actively to the repeated impression which forces itself on our memory with increased vividness on account of this active personal reaction.

We may consider how such factors can be tested by the psychotechnical experiment. Scott, for instance, studied the direct influence of the relative size of the advertisements.[50] He constructed a book of a hundred pages from advertisements which had been cut from various magazines and which referred to many different articles. Fifty persons who did not know anything about the purpose of the experiment had to glance over the pages of the book as they would look though the advertising parts of a monthly. The time which they used for it was about ten minutes. As soon as they had gone through the hundred pages, they were asked to write down what they remembered. The result from this method was that the 50 persons mentioned on an average every full-page advertisement $6\frac{1}{2}$ times, every half-page less than 3 times, every fourth-page a little more than 1 time, and the still smaller advertisements only about $\frac{1}{7}$ time. This series of experiments suggested accordingly that the memory value of a fourth-page advertisement is much smaller than one fourth of the memory-value of a full-page advertisement, and that of an eighth-page again much smaller than one half of the psychical value of a fourth-page. The customer who pays for one eighth of a page receives not the eighth part, but hardly the twentieth part of the psychical influence which is produced by a full page.

These experiments, which were carried on in various forms, demanded as a natural supplement a study of the effects of repetition in relation to size. This was the object of a series of tests which I carried on recently in the Harvard laboratory. I constructed the following material: 60 sheets of Bristol board in folio size were covered with advertisements which were cut from magazines the size of the "Saturday Evening Post" and the "Ladies' Home Journal." We used advertisements ranging from full-page to twelfth-page in size. Every one of the 6 full-page advertisements which we used occurred only once, each of the 12 half-page advertisements was given 2 times, each of the fourth-page size, 4 times, each of the eighth-page size, 8 times, and each of the twelfth-page size, 12 times. The repetitions were cut from 12 copies of the magazine number. The same advertisement never occurred on the same page; every page, unless it was covered by a full-page advertisement, offered a combination of various announcements. It is evident that by this arrangement every single advertisement occupied the same space, as the 8 times repeated eighth-page advertisement filled a full page too. Thus no one of the 60 announcements which we used was spatially favored above another.

Thirty persons took part in the experiment. Each one had to devote himself to the 60 pages in such a way that every page was looked at for exactly 20 seconds. Between each two pages was a pause of 3 seconds, sufficient to allow one sheet to be laid aside and the next to be grasped. In 23 minutes the whole series had been gone through, and immediately after that every one had to write down what he remembered, both the names of the firms and the article announced. In the cases where only the name or only the article was correctly remembered, the result counted $\frac{1}{2}$. We found great individual differences, probably not only because the memory of the different persons was different, but also because they varied in the degree of interest with which they looked at such material. The smallest number of reproductions was 18, of which 14 were only half remembered, that is, only the name or only the article, and as we counted these half reproductions $\frac{1}{2}$, the memory-value for this person was counted 11. The maximum reproduction was 46, of which 6 were half remembered.

If these calculated values are added and the sum divided by the number of participants, that is, 30, and this finally by the number of the advertisements shown, that is, 60, we obtain the average memory-value of a single advertisement. The results showed that this was 0.44. But our real interest referred to the distribution for the advertisements of different size. If we make the same calculation, not for the totality of the advertisements but for those of a particular size, we find that the memory-value for the full-page advertisement was 0.33, for the 2 times repeated half-page advertisement, 0.30, for the 4 times repeated fourth-page advertisement 0.49, for the 8 times repeated eighth-page advertisement, 0.44, and for the 12 times repeated twelfth-page advertisement, 0.47. Hence we come to the result that the 4 times repeated fourth-page advertisement as $1\frac{1}{2}$ times stronger memory-value than one offering of a full-page, or the 2 times repeated half-page, but that this relation does not grow with a further reduction of the size. Two thirds of the subjects were men and one third women. On the whole, the same relation exists for both groups, but the climax of psychical efficiency was reached in the case of the men by the 4 times repeated fourth-page, in the case of the women by the 8 times repeated eighth-page. The 4 times repeated fourth-page in the case of the women was 0.45, in the case of the men, 0.51, the 8 times repeated eighth-page, women, 0.53, men, 0.37.

I am inclined to believe that the ascent of the curve of the memory-value from the full-page to the fourth-page or eighth-page would have been still more continuous, if the whole-page advertisements had not naturally been such as are best known to the American reader. The whole-page announcement, therefore, had a certain natural advantage. But when we come to another calculation, even the effect of this advantage is lost. We examined the relations for the first 10 names and articles, which every one of the 30 persons wrote down. These first 10 were mostly dashed down quickly without special thought. They also included only a few half reproductions. When we study these 300 answers which the 30 persons wrote as their first 10 reproductions, and calculate from them the chances which every one of the 60 advertisements had for being remembered, we obtain the following values: The probability of being remembered among the first 10 was for the full-page advertisement, 0.5, for the half-page 2 times repeated, 1.2, for the fourth-page 4 times repeated, 2.9, for the eighth-page 8 times repeated,

2.3, and for the twelfth-page 12 times repeated, 2.4. The superiority of repetition over mere size appears most impressively in this form, but we see again in this series that the effect decreases even with increased number of repetitions as soon as the single advertisement sinks below a certain relative size, so that the 12 times repeated twelfth-page advertisement does not possess the memory-value of the 4 times repeated fourth-page advertisement. If Scott's experiments concerning the size and these experiments of mine concerning the repetition are right, the memory-value of the advertisements for economic purposes is dependent upon complicated conditions. A business man who brings out a full-page advertisement once in a paper which has 100,000 readers would leave the desired memory-impression on a larger number of individuals than if he were to print a fourth-page advertisement in four different cities in four local papers, each of which has 100,000 readers. But if he uses the same paper in one town, he would produce a much greater effect by printing a fourth of a page four times than by using a full-page advertisement once only.

As a matter of course this would hold true only as far as size and repetition are concerned. Many other factors have to be considered besides. Some of these could even be studied with our material.

THE EFFECTS OF ADVERTISEMENTS

We could study from our results what memory-value is attached to the various forms of type or suggestive words, what influence to illustrations, how far they reinforce the impressiveness and how far they draw away the attention from the name and the object, how these various factors influence men and women differently, and so on. Other questions, however, demand entirely different forms of experiment. We may examine the effects of special contrast phenomena, of unusual background, of irregular borders and original headings. The particular position of the advertisement also deserves our psychological interest. The magazines receive higher prices for the cover pages and the newspapers for advertisements which are surrounded by reading matter. In both cases obvious practical motives are decisive. The cover page comes into the field of vision more frequently. What is surrounded by reading matter is less easily overlooked.

But the newspaper world hardly realizes how much other variations of position influence the psychological effect. Starch [51] made experiments in which he did not use real advertisements, but meaningless syllables so as to exclude the influence of familiarity with any announcement. He arranged little booklets, each of 12 pages, on which a syllable such as *lod, zan, mep, dut, yib,* and so on was printed in the middle of each page. Each of his 50 subjects glanced over the book and then wrote down what syllables remained in memory. He found that the syllables which stood on the first and last page were remembered by 34 persons, those on the second and eleventh by about 26, and those on the eight other pages by an average of 17 persons. In the next experiment he printed one syllable in the middle of the upper and one in the middle of the lower half of each page. The results now showed that of those syllables which were remembered 54 per cent stood on the upper half and 46 per cent on the lower half of the page. Finally, he divided every page into four parts and printed one syllable on the middle of each fourth of a page. The results showed that of the remembered syllables 28 per cent stood on the left-hand upper fourth, 33 per cent on the right-hand upper fourth, 16 per cent left-hand lower, and 23 per cent right-hand lower. A fourth-page advertisement which is printed on the outer side of the upper half of the page thus probably has more than twice the psychological value of one which is printed on the inner side of the lower half. The economic world spends millions every year for advertisements on the upper right-hand side and millions for advertisements on the lower left-hand side, and is not aware that one represents twice the value of the other. These little illustrations of advertisement experiments may suffice to indicate how much haphazard methods are still prevalent in the whole field of economic psychotechnics, methods which would not be tolerated in the sphere of physical and chemical technology.

XXI

THE EFFECT OF DISPLAY

IF we turn from the simple newspaper advertisement to the means of propaganda in general, we at once stand before a question which is
often wrongly answered. The practical handbooks
of advertisements and means of display treat
it as a self-evident fact that every presentation
should be as beautiful as possible. In the first
place, we cannot deny that the ugly and even the
disgusting possess a strong power for attracting
attention. Yet it is true that by a transposition of
feelings the displeasure in the advertisement may
easily become a displeasure in the advertised object. But, on the other hand, it is surely a mistake to believe that pure beauty best fulfills the
function of the advertisement. Even the drafts-
man who draws a poster ought to give up the am-
bition to create a perfect picture. It might have
the power to attract attention, but it would
hardly serve its true purpose of fixing the attention on the article which is advertised by the
picture. The very meaning of beauty lies in its
self-completeness. The beautiful picture rests
in itself and does not point beyond itself. A really

beautiful landscape painting is an end in itself, and must not stir up the practical wish to visit the landscape which has stimulated the eye of the painter. If the display is to serve economic interests, every line and every curve, every form and every color, must be subordinated to the task of leading to a practical resolution, and to an action, and yet this is exactly the opposite of the meaning of art. Art must inhibit action, if it is perfect. The artist is not to make us believe that we deal with a real object which suggests a practical attitude. The æsthetic forms are adjusted to the main æsthetic aim, the inhibition of practical desires. The display must be pleasant, tasteful, harmonious, and suggestive, but should not be beautiful, if it is to fulfill its purpose in the fullest sense. It loses its economic value, if by its artistic quality it oversteps the boundaries of that middle region of arts and crafts. This of course stands in no contradiction to the requirement that the advertised article should be made to appear as beautiful as possible. The presentation of something beautiful is not necessarily a beautiful presentation, just as a perfectly beautiful picture need not have something beautiful as its content. A perfect painting may be the picture of a most ugly person.

We have not yet spoken of the suggestive

273

power of the means of propaganda. Every one knows how the influence on taste and smell, on social vanity, on local pride, on the gambling instinct, on the instinctive fear of diseases, and above all on the sexual instinct, can gain suggestive power. Everywhere among the uncritical masses such appeals reach individuals whose psychophysical attitudes make such influences vivid and overpowering. Every one knows, too, those often clever linguistic forms which are to aid the suggestion. They are to inhibit the opposing impulses. The mere use of the imperative, to be sure, has gradually become an ineffective, used-up pattern. It is a question for special economic psychotechnics to investigate how the suggestive strength of a form can be reinforced or weakened by various secondary influences. What influence, for example, belongs to the electric sign advertisements in which the sudden change from light to darkness produces strong psychophysical effects, and what value belongs to moving parts in the picture?

The psychologist takes the same interest in the examples of window displays, sample distributions, and similar vehicles of commerce by which the offered articles themselves and not their mere picture or description are to influence the consciousness of the prospective customer.

Here, too, every element may be isolated and may be brought under psychotechnical rules. The most external question would refer to the mere quantity of the presented material. The psychologist would ask how the mere mass of the offering influences the attention, how far the feeling of pleasure in the fullness, how far the æsthetic impression of repetition, how far the associative thought of a manifold selection, how far the mere spatial expansion, affects the impression. In any case, as soon as it is acknowledged as desirable to produce with certain objects the impression of the greatest possible number, the experimental psychologist stands before the concrete problem of how a manifoldness of things is to be distributed so that it will not be underestimated, perhaps even overestimated as to quantity. Again, the laboratory experiment would not proceed with real window displays or real exhibitions, but would work out the principle with the simplified experimental means.

An investigation in the Harvard laboratory, for instance, tested the influence which various factors have upon the estimation of a number of objects seen.[52] The question was how far the form or the size or the distribution makes a group of objects appear larger or smaller. The experiment was started by showing 20 small cards on a black background in comparison with another group of cards the number of which varied between 17 and 23. At first the form of these little cards was changed: triangles, squares, and circles were tried. Or the color was changed: light and dark, saturated and unsaturated colors were used. Or the order was varied: sometimes the little cards lay in regular rows, sometimes in close clusters, sometimes widely distributed, sometimes in quite irregular fashion. Or the background was changed, or the surrounding frame, or the time of exposure, and so on. Each time the subjects had to estimate whether the second group was the larger or equal or the smaller. These experiments indicated that such comparative estimation was indeed influenced by every one of the factors mentioned. If the experiments show that an irregular distribution makes the number appear larger or a close clustering reduces the apparent number, and so on, the business man would be quite able to profit from such knowledge. The jeweler who shows his rings and watches in his window wishes to produce with his small stock the impression of an ample supply. He lacks the psychology which might teach him whether he would act more wisely in having the rings and the watches separated, or whether he should mix the two, whether he ought to choose a background which is similar in color or one which contrasts with the pieces exhibited, whether he ought to present the single object in a special background as in a case, or to show it without one. He is not aware that by simple psychological illusions, it is not difficult to change the apparent size of an isolated object by special treatment, making his show-piece appear larger by a fitting background or intentionally making a dainty object appear smaller by contrasting surroundings. These, to be sure, are very trivial illustrations, but the same fundamental psychological laws which are true for the show-window of the next corner store are true for the world-display of the nation. The point is to present clearly the idea, which can be most simply expressed in such trivial material. But it may be added that even in the case of the most indifferent example a few hasty experiments with one or two subjects cannot yield any results of value.

All parts of physiological psychological optics can contribute similar material. The questions of color harmony and color contrast, light intensity and mutual support of uniformly colored objects, of irradiation, depth and perspective, are significant for an effective display in the show-window, and the laboratory results can easily be translated into psychotechnical prescriptions.

THE BEST POSSIBLE EFFECT

But here it is still more necessary to separate carefully the merely optical aspect of the impression from its æsthetic side. All that we claimed as to the poster is still more justified for the presentation of the saleable objects themselves. As soon as the display of the articles forms a real work of art, it must produce inhibitions in the soul of the spectator by which the practical economic desire is turned aside. Beauty here too has strong power of attraction, and moreover the suggestive power, by which it withdraws our senses from the chance surroundings, forces us to lose ourselves in the offered presentation. But just through this process the content of the display becomes isolated and separated from the world of our practical interests. Our desires are brought to silence, we do not seek a personal relation to the things which we face as admiring spectators, and the intended economic effect is therefore eliminated. Whoever is to examine the psychotechnics of displays and exhibitions must therefore study the psychology of æsthetic stimulation, of suggestion, of the effects of light, color, form and movement, of apperception and attention, and ought not to forget the psychology of humor and curiosity, of instincts and emotions. For us the essential point is that here too the experimental psychological method alone is able to lead from mere chance arrangements founded on personal taste to the systematic construction which secures with the greatest possible certainty the greatest possible mental effect in the service of the economic purpose.

The problems of the storekeeper who arranges his windows, however, overlap the problems of the manufacturer who prepares his goods for the world-market, and who must from the start take care that the outer appearance of his goods stimulate the readiness to buy. In factories in which these questions have been carefully considered, the psychological elements have always been found to be the most influential, but often the most puzzling. I received material from a number of industrial plants which sold the same article in a variety of packings. The material which was sent to me included all kinds of soaps and candies, writing-papers and breakfast foods, and other articles which are handled by the retailer, the sale of which depends upon the inclination and caprice of the customer in the store. For every one of these objects a number of external covers and labels were sent and with them a confidential report with details about their relative success. For instance, a certain kind of chocolate was sold under 12 different labels. One of them was highly successful in the whole country, and one

other had made the same article entirely unsale-
able. The other 10 could be graded between these
extremes. In all 12 cases the covers were deco-
rated with pictures of women with a scenic background. As long as only æsthetic values were
considered, all were on nearly the same level,
and æsthetically skilled observers repeatedly expressed their preference for some of the unsuccessful pictures over some of the successful ones. But
as soon as an internal relation was formed between
the pictures and the chocolate, in the one case a
mental harmony resulted which had strong suggestive power, in the other case a certain unrest
and inner disturbance which necessarily had an
inhibiting influence. The picture which was unsuccessful with the sweets would perhaps have
been eminently successful for tobacco. From
such elementary starting-points, the laboratory
experiment might proceed systematically into
spheres of economic life hitherto untouched by
scientific methods. The psychology of the influence of external forms on the conscious reactions
of the masses is so far usually considered only
when, as often happens, the most fundamental
demands are violated; for instance, when objects
which are to give the impression of ease are
painted in colors which give a heavy, clumsy appearance, or vice versa, when book-bindings are

THE EFFECT OF DISPLAY

lettered in archaic type which makes the reading of the title impossible for a passer-by, and many similar antipsychological absurdities which any stroll through the streets of a modern city forces on us.

XXII

EXPERIMENTS WITH REFERENCE TO ILLEGAL IMITATION

IT is perhaps not without interest to turn into a by-path at this point of our road. All the illustrations which we have picked out so far have referred to strictly economic conditions. But we ought not to forget that these economic problems of commerce and industry are everywhere in contact with legal interests as well. In order to indicate the manifoldness of problems accessible to the experimental method, we may discuss our last question, the question of packing and of labels, in this legal relation too. All the packings, covers, labels, trademarks, and names by which the manufacturer tries to stimulate the attention, the imagination, and the suggestibility of the customer may easily draw a large part of their psychological effectiveness from without, as soon as they imitate the appearance of articles which are well introduced and favored in the market. If the public is familiar with and favorably inclined toward an article on account of its inner values or on account of its being much advertised, a similar name or a similar packing may offer efficient help to a rival article. The law of course protects the label and the deceiving imitation can be prosecuted. But no law can determine by general conceptions the exact point at which the similarity becomes legally unallowable. This creates a situation which has given rise to endless difficulties in practical life.

If everything were forbidden which by its similarity to an accredited article might lead to a possible confusion in the mind of the quite careless and inattentive customer, any article once in the market would have a monopoly in its line. As soon as a typewriter or an automobile or a pencil or a mineral water existed, no second kind could have access to the market, as with a high degree of carelessness one economic rival may be taken for another, even if the new typewriter or the new pencil has a new form and color and name. On the other side, the purchaser could never have a feeling of security if imitations were considered as still legally justifiable when the difference is so small that it needs an intense mental effort and careful examination of details to notice it.

The result is that the jurisdiction fluctuates between these two extremes in a most alarming way, and this seems to hold true in all countries. In

theory: "There is substantial agreement that infringement occurs when the marks, names, labels, or packings of one trader resemble those of
another sufficiently to make it probable that ordinary purchasers, exercising no more care than
such persons usually do in purchasing the article
in question, will be deceived." But it depends
upon the trade experts and the judges to give
meaning to such a statement in the particular
case, as the amount of care which purchasers
usually exercise can be understood very differently. Sometimes the customer is expected to
proceed with an attention which is most subtly
adjusted to the finest differences, and sometimes
it is taken for granted that he is unable to notice
even strong variations. It is clear that this uncertainty which disturbs the whole trade cannot
be eliminated as long as the psychological background has not been systematically studied.
Mere talking about the attention of the customer,
and his ability to decide and select, and of his observations and his habits in the spirit of popular
common-sense psychology, can never secure exact
standards and definite demarcation lines. The
question is important not only where imitations
of morally doubtful character are in the market.
Even the most honest manufacturer is in a certain sense obliged to imitate his predecessors,

as they have directed the taste and habits of the public in particular directions, and as the product of his company would suffer unnecessarily if he were to disregard this psychical attitude of the prospective customers. The economic legal situation accordingly suggests the question whether it would not be possible to devise methods for an exact measurement of the permissible similarity, and this demand for exactitude naturally points to the methods of the psychological experiment. E. S. Rogers, Esq., of Chicago, who has thoroughly discussed the legal aspect of the problem,[53] first turned my attention to the psychological difficulty involved.

When I approached the question in the Harvard psychological laboratory, it was clear to me that the degree of attention and carefulness which the court may presuppose on the part of the customer can never be determined by the psychologist and his experimental methods. It would be meaningless, if we tried to discover by experiments a particular degree of similarity which every one ought to recognize or a particular degree of attention which would be sufficient for protection against fraud. Such degrees must always remain dependent upon arbitrary decision. They are not settled by natural conditions, but are entirely dependent upon social agreement. A decision outside of the realm of psychology must fix upon a particular degree in the scale of various similarity values as the limit which is not to be passed. The aim of the psychologist can be only to construct such a scale by which decisions may be made comparable and by which standards may become possible. The experiment cannot deduce from the study of mental phenomena what degrees of similarity ought to be still admissible, but it may be able to develop methods by which different degrees of similarity can be discriminated and by which a certain similarity value once selected can always be found again with objective certainty. After many fruitless efforts I settled on the following form of experiments, which I hope may bring us nearer to the attainment of the purpose.

A group of objects is observed for a definite time and after a definite interval another group of objects is offered for comparison. This second group is identical with the first in all but one of the objects, and this is replaced by a similar one. The question is how often this substitution will be noticed by the observers. I may give in detail a characterization of the set of experiments in which we are at present engaged. We are working with picture postal cards, using many hundred cards of different kinds, but for each one we have one or several similar cards. As postal cards are generally manufactured in sets, it is not difficult to purchase pairs of pictures with any degree of similarity. Two cards with Christmas trees, or two with Easter eggs, or two with football players, or two with forest landscapes, and so on, may differ all the way from a slight variation of color or a hardly noticeable change in the position of details to variations which keep the same motive or the same general arrangement, but after all make the card strikingly different. The first step is to determine for each pair the degree of similarity, on a percentage basis. To overcome mere arbitrariness, we ask thirty to forty educated persons to express the similarity value, calling identical postal cards 100 per cent and two postal cards as different as a colored flower piece and a black picture of a street scene 0. The average value of these judgments is then considered as expressing the objective degree of similarity between the two pictures of a pair. After securing such standard values, we carry on the experiments in the following form. Six different postal cards, for instance, are seen on a black background through the opening of a shutter which is closed after 5 seconds. The six may be made up of a landscape, a building, a head, a genre scene, and so forth. After 20 seconds the same group of postal cards is shown once more, except that one is replaced by a similar one, instead of one church another church building, or instead of a vase with roses a vase with pi: 's. If the substituted picture has the average similarity value of 80 per cent and we make the experiment with 10 persons, the substitution may be discovered by 7 persons and remain unnoticed by 3. We can now easily vary every one of the factors involved. If instead of 6 cards, we take 10, it may be that only 4 out of 10 persons, instead of 7, will discover the substitution, while if we take 4 cards instead of 6, perhaps 9 persons out of 10 will recognize the difference under these otherwise equal conditions. Only an especially careless observer will overlook it. But instead of changing the number of objects, we may change the periods of exposure. If we show the 6 cards only for 2 seconds instead of 5 seconds, the number of those who recognize the difference may sink from 7 to 5 or 4, and if we make the time considerably longer, we shall of course reach a point where all 10 will recognize the substitution. The same holds true of the shortening or lengthening of the time-interval between the two presentations. The third variable factor is the similarity itself. If instead of one church, not another church, but a theatre or a skyscraper is shown, that is, if the similarity value of 80 per cent sinks down to a similarity of 60 per cent or 50 per cent, the number of those who recognize the substitution will again become larger; if, on the other hand, the substituted card shows the same church, only from a slightly different angle, bringing the similarity value up to 90 per cent or 95 per cent, the number of observers who recognize the substitution may sink to 2 or 3. To make the experiments reliable, it is also necessary frequently to mix in cases in which no substitution at all is introduced.

If these experiments are varied sufficiently and a large mass of material brought together, we must be able to secure definite formulæ. We may find that if the critical card appears among 6 cards, is shown for 5 seconds, and the group is again exposed after 20 seconds, 80 per cent of the subjects will recognize the substitution of a similar card, if the degree of similarity is 30 per cent, but only 60 per cent will recognize it if the degree of similarity is 70 per cent, and only 30 per cent will recognize it if the degree of similarity is 90 per cent. These are entirely fictitious figures and are only to indicate the principle. If such an exact formula were definitely discovered, we should still be unable to say from mere psychological reasoning what similarity value is legally permissible. If the rules against infringement are interpreted in a very rigorous spirit, it may seem desirable to prohibit imitations which are as little similar as those postal cards which were graded as 40 per cent in our similarity scale, and if the interpretation is a loose one, it may appear permissible to have imitations on the market which are as strongly similar as our postal cards graded at 80 per cent in our similarity scale. All this would have to be left to the lawmakers and to the judges. But what we would have gained is this. We could say: if our object exposed for 5 seconds in a group of 6 other objects is replaced after an interval of 20 seconds by an imitation and this change is recognized by 8 persons among 10, the degree of similarity is 30 per cent and if it is recognized by 3 out of 10 subjects, the degree of similarity is 90 per cent. In short, from any percentage of subjects who under these conditions discovered the substitution, we could determine the degree of similarity, independent of any individual arbitrariness. If such methods were accepted by the trade and the courts, it would only be necessary to agree on the percentage of similarity which ought to be permitted, and all uncertainty would disappear. There would be no wrangling of opposing interests; it would be possible to find out whether the permitted limit were overstepped or not with an exactitude similar to that with which the weight or the chemical constitution of a trade commodity is examined. Certainly the experiment establishes here conditions which are very different from those of practical life. The customer who wants to buy a particular picture postal card which he saw once before and to whom the salesman offers a similar one, suggesting that it is the same, is facing only one card and not a group of six. But in practical life the card which he has seen was not observed with the definite intention of keeping the memory picture in mind, and months may have passed since it was seen. The memory picture which the customer has in his consciousness when he seeks the particular card is much weakened by this circumstance too. We secure this weakening artificially by the arrangement of the experiment in placing the card in a group of six or ten and exposing them for a few seconds only. The force of attention and the corresponding memory-value are by this distribution diminished in a definite degree in the case of every single card.

The investigation must include a careful study of the size of the groups, of the time-relations, of the percentage of correct answers, all under the point of view of greatest fitness for practical application. In the Harvard laboratory the research has been carried on partly with such picture material, partly with word material, and partly with concrete objects.[54] Whatever the details of the outcome may be, we hope that the work will lead to results which may, indeed, make such a psychotechnical use possible. Its principles and formulæ might easily be adjusted to any marketable material. As a matter of course, if in future the courts were ever to accept such psychological, experimental methods, it would be intolerable dilettantism if such experiments were carried on by lawyers and district attorneys. It is as true of this economic legal question as of many other legal psychological problems that its introduction into the courtroom can become desirable only when psychological experts are engaged and called in the same way as chemical or medical experts are invited to the court. On the other hand, there is surely not the slightest desire on the part of psychologists to be dragged into humiliating performances like those which not only handwriting experts, but even psychiatric specialists have had to undergo repeatedly in sensational court trials. The day for the expert activity in the courtroom will come for the psychologist only when the country has attached the expert to the court and has eliminated the expert retained by the plaintiff or the defendant. But this general

ILLEGAL IMITATION

practical question as to the position of the psychologist in the courtroom and as to the need of a
psychological laboratory in connection with the
courts would lead us too far aside.

XXIII

BUYING AND SELLING

THE effects which we have studied so far were produced by inanimate objects, posters or displays, advertisements or labels and packings. The economic psychotechnics of the future will surely study with similar methods the effects of the living commercial agencies. Experiments will trace the exact effects which the salesman or customer may produce. But here not even a modest beginning can be discovered, and it would be difficult to mention a single example of experimental research. The desired psychological influences of the salesman are not quite dissimilar to those of the printed means of propaganda. Here, too, it is essential to turn the attention of the customer to different points, to awaken a vivid favorable impression, to emphasize the advantages of the goods, to throw full light on them, and finally to influence the will-decision either by convincing arguments or by persuasion and suggestion. In either case the point is to enhance the impulse to buy and to suppress the opposing ideas. Yet every one of these factors, when it starts from a man and not from a thing or paper, changes its form. The influence becomes narrower, it is directed toward a smaller number of persons; but, on the other hand, it gains just by the new possibility of individualization. The salesman in the store or the commercial traveler adjusts himself to the wishes, reactions, and replies of the buyer. Above all, when it becomes necessary to direct the attention to the decisive points, the personal agent has the possibility of developing the whole process through a series of stages so that the attention slowly becomes focused on one definite point. The salesman observes at first only the general limits of the interest of the customer as far as it is indicated by his reactions, but slowly he can find out in this whole field the region of strongest desires. As soon as he has discovered this narrower region in which the prospects of success seem to be greatest, he can systematically eliminate everything which distracts and scatters the attention. He can discover whether the psyche of the individual with whom he is dealing can be influenced more strongly by logical arguments or by suggestion, and how far he may calculate on the pleasure instincts, on the excitement of emotions, on the impulse to imitate, on the natural vanity, on the desire for saving, and on the longing for luxury. In every one of these directions the whole play of human suggestion may be helpful.

THE BEST POSSIBLE EFFECT

The voice may win or destroy confidence, the statement may by its firmness overcome counter-motives or by its uncertainty reinforce them. Even hand or arm movements by their motor suggestion may focus the desires of the customers, while unskillful, erratic movements may scatter the attention and lead to an inner oscillation of the will to buy.

At every one of these points the psychological experiment may find a foothold, and only through such methodological study can the haphazard proceedings of the commercial world be transformed into really economic schemes. Indeed, it seems nothing but chance that just this field is controlled by chance alone. The enormous social interplay of energies which are discharged in the selling and buying of the millions becomes utterly planless as soon as salesman and customer come into contact, and this tremendous waste of energy cannot appear desirable for any possible interest of civilization. The time alone which is wasted by useless psychophysical operations in front of and behind the counter represents a gigantic part of the national budget. Even the complaints about the long working day of the salesgirls might be eliminated from the debit account of the national ledger, if the commercial companies could study the psychical processes in selling and buying with the same carefulness with which they analyze all details in preparing the stock and fixing the prices. In the army or in the fire department, in the railroad service, and even in the factory, all necessary activities are so arranged that as far as possible the greatest achievement is secured by the smallest amount of energy. But when the hundreds of millions of customers in the civilized world want to satisfy their economic demands in the stores, the whole dissolves into a flood of talk, because no one has taken the trouble to examine scientifically the psychotechnics of selling and to put it on a firm psychological foundation.

The idea of scientific management must be extended from the industrial concerns to the commercial establishments. The questioning and answering, the showing and replacing of the goods, the demonstrating and suggesting by the salesmen, must be brought into an economic system which saves time and energy, as has been tried with the laborer in the factory. Wherever economic processes are carried out with superfluous, haphazard movements, the national resources have to suffer a loss. The single individual can never find the ideal form of motion and the ideal process by mere instinct. A systematic investigation is needed to determine the way to the greatest saving of energy, and the result ought to be made a binding rule for every apprentice. How the smallest influences grow by summation may be illustrated by the experience of a large department store, in which the expense for delivery of the articles sold was felt as too large an item in the budget. The hundreds of saleswomen therefore received the order after every sale of moderate-sized articles not to ask, as before, "May we send it to you?" but instead, "Will you take it with you?" Probably none of the many thousand daily customers observed the difference, the more as it was indifferent to most of them whether they took the little package home themselves or not. In cases in which it was inconvenient, they would anyhow oppose the suggestion and insist that the purchase be sent to them. Yet it is claimed that this hardly noticeable suggestion led to a considerable saving in the following year, distinctly felt in the budget of the whole establishment.

We must not forget, however, that the process of buying deserves the same psychological interest as that of selling. If psychotechnics is to be put into the service of a valuable economic task, the goal cannot possibly be to devise schemes by which the customer may easily be trapped. The purpose of science cannot be to help any one to sell articles to a man who does not need them and who would regret the purchase after quiet thought. The applied psychologist should help the prospective buyer no less, and must protect him so that his true intention may become realized in the economic process. Otherwise through his suggestibility, the determining idea of his goal might fade in his consciousness and the appeal to his vanity or to his instincts might awaken an anti-economic desire which he would be too weak to inhibit. The salesman must know how to use arguments and suggestions and how to make them effective,[55] but the customer too must know how to see through a misleading argument and how to resist mere suggestion.

The postulate that the psychical factors in commercial life are to be carefully regarded is repeated in more complex form in the wholesale business and in the stock exchange. It is a perfectly justified and consistent thought which recently led a large credit bureau to an effort to base its information on psychological analysis. It is well known that there are bureaus in which the ledger experiences of a large circle of companies in the same commercial line are collected, tabulated, and recorded, thus affording an automatic review of the occurrences, focusing early attention on doubtful accounts and pointing out weaknesses in the customers' conditions, as they develop, as well as evidences of prosperity. The ledger experience which a single company has with all its customers is tabulated without revealing its identity to the associates, who get reports containing it, and the many combined ledgers become a valuable guide. Yet all such methods can show only actual movements in the market, and cannot allow the prospects of future development to be determined, simply because they cannot take into account the personal equations. Only an acquaintance with the character and the temperament, the intelligence and the habits, the energy and the weakness, of the head of a firm can tell us whether the company, even with satisfactory resources, may go down, or whether, even though embarrassed, it may hold out. The psychological pioneer, therefore, aims not only toward an exchange of ledger accounts, but toward a real psychological diagnosis and prognosis. If a member of a firm is personally known to some scores of business men' who have had commercial dealings with him, and each one of them, without disclosing his identity to any one but the central bureau, sends to it a statement of personal impressions, a composite picture of the mental physiognomy can be worked out. Of course all this has been often done in the terms of popular psychology and in a haphazard, amateurish way. The new plan is to arrange the questions systematically under the point of view of scientific descriptive psychology. Regular psychograms, in which the probability of a particular kind of behavior is to be determined in an exact percentage calculation, are to replace the traditional vagueness, as soon as a sufficient number of reliable answers have been tabulated.

Commercial life as a whole finds its contact with psychology, of course, not only in the problem of how to secure the best mental effect. Those other questions which we have discussed essentially with reference to factory life and industrial concerns, namely, how the best man and the best work are to be secured, recur in the circle of commercial endeavors. It seems, indeed, most desirable to devise psychological tests by which the ability to be a successful salesman or saleswoman may be determined at an early stage. The lamentable shifting of the employees in all commercial spheres, with its injurious social consequences, would then be unnecessary, and both employers and employees would profit. Moreover, like the selection of the men, the means of securing the most satisfactory work from them, has also so far been left entirely to common sense. Commercial work stands under an abundance of varying conditions, and each may have influences the isolated effects of which are not known, because they have not been studied in that systematic form which only the experiment can establish. The popular literature on this whole group of subjects is extensive, and in its expansion corresponds to the widespread demand for real information and advice to the salesman. But hardly any part of the literature in the borderland regions of economics is so disappointing in its vagueness, emptiness, and helplessness. Experimental psychology has nothing with which to replace it to-day, but it can at least show the direction from which decisive help may be expected in future.

XXIV

THE FUTURE DEVELOPMENT OF ECONOMIC PSYCHOLOGY

HERE we may stop. From those elementary questions concerning the mental effects, the path would quickly lead to questions of gravest importance. What is the mental effect which the economic labor produces in the laborer himself? How do economic movements influence the mind of the community? How far do non-economic factors produce effects on the psychical mechanism of the economic agents? But it would be idle to claim to-day for exact psychology, with its methods of causal thought, regions in which so far popular psychology, with its methods of purposive thought, is still sovereign. Our aim certainly was not to review the totality of possible problems related to economic efficiency, but merely to demonstrate the principles and the methods of experimental economic psychology by a few characteristic illustrations. As all the examples which we selected were chosen only in order to make clear the characteristic point of view of psychotechnics, it is unimportant whether the particular results will stand the test of further experimental investigations, or will have to be modified by new researches. What is needed to-day is not to distribute the results so far reached as if they were parts of a definite knowledge, but only to emphasize that the little which has been accomplished should encourage continuous effort. To stimulate such further work is the only purpose of this sketch.

This further work will have to be a work of cooperation. The nature of this problem demands a relatively large number of persons for the experimental treatment. With most experimental researches in our psychological laboratories, the number of the subjects experimented on is not so important as the number of experiments made with a few well-trained participants. But with the questions of applied psychology the number of persons plays a much more significant rôle, as the individual differences become of greatest import-ance. The same problems ought therefore to be studied in various places, so that the results may be exchanged and compared. Moreover, these psychological economic investigations naturally lead beyond the possibilities of the university laboratories. To a certain degree this was true of other parts of applied psychology as well. Educational and medical experimental psychology could not reach their fullest productivity until

the experiment was systematically carried into
the schoolroom and the psychiatric clinic. But
the classroom and the hospital are relatively accessible places for the scientific worker, as both
are anyhow conducted under a scientific point of
view. The teacher and the physician can easily
learn to perform valuable experiments with
school children or with patients. This favorable
condition is lacking in the workshop and the factory, in the banks and the markets. The acade-
mic psychologist will be able to undertake work
there only with a very disturbing expenditure of
time and only under exceptional conditions. If
such experiments, for instance, with laborers in
a factory or employees of a railway are to advance beyond the faint first efforts of to-day and
are really to become serviceable to the cultural
progress of our time with effective completeness,
they ought not to remain an accidental appendix
to the theoretical laboratories. Either the uni-
versities must create special laboratories for
applied psychology or independent research institutes must be founded which attack the new
concrete problems under the point of view of
national political economy. Experimental workshops could be created which are really adjusted
to the special practical needs and to which a
sufficiently large number of persons could be

drawn for the systematic researches. The ideal solution for the United States would be a governmental bureau for applied psychology, with special reference to the psychology of commerce and industry, similar to the model agricultural stations all over the land under the Department of Agriculture.

Only when such a broad foundation has been secured will the time be ripe to carry the method systematically into the daily work. The aim will never be for real experimental researches to be performed by the foreman in the workshop or by the superintendent in the factory. But slowly a certain acknowledged system of rules and prescriptions may be worked out which may be used as patterns, and which will not presuppose any scientific knowledge, any more than an understanding of the principles of electricity is necessary for one who uses the telephone. But besides the rigid rules which any one may apply, particular prescriptions will be needed fitting the special situation. This leads to the demand for the large establishments to appoint professionally trained psychologists who will devote their services to the psychological problems of the special industrial plant. There are many factories that have scores of scientifically trained chemists or physicists at work, but who would consider it an unproductive luxury to appoint a scientifically schooled experimental psychologist to their staff. And yet his observations and researches might become economically the most important factor. Similar expectations might be justified for the large department stores and especially for the big transportation companies. In smaller dimensions the same real needs exist in the ordinary workshop and store. It is obvious that the professional consulting psychologist would satisfy these needs most directly, and if such a new group of engineers were to enter into industrial life, very soon a further specialization might be expected. Some of these psychological engineers would devote themselves to the problems of vocational selection and appointment; others would specialize on questions of advertisement and display and propaganda; a third group on problems of fatigue, efficiency, and recreation; a fourth on the psychological demands for the arrangement of the machines; and every day would give rise to new divisions. Such a well-schooled specialist, if he spent a few hours in a workshop or a few days in a factory, could submit propositions which might refer exclusively to the psychological factors and yet which might be more important for the earning and the profit of the establishment than the mere buying of new machines or the mere increase in the number of laborers.

No one can deny that such a transition must be burdened with difficult complications and even with dangers; and still less will any one doubt that it may be caricatured. One who demands that a chauffeur or a motorman of an electric railway be examined as to his psychical abilities by systematic psychological methods, so that accidents may be avoided, does not necessarily demand that a congressman or a cabinet minister or a candidate for marriage be tested too by psychological laboratory experiments, as the witty ones have proposed. And one who believes that the work in the factory ought to be studied with reference to the smallest possible expenditure of psychical impulses is not convinced that the same experimental methods will be necessary for the functions of eating and drinking and love-making, as has been suggested.

And if it is true that difficulties and discomforts are to be feared during the transition period, they should be more than outweighed by the splendid betterments to be hoped for. We must not forget that the increase of industrial efficiency by future psychological adaptation and by improvement of the psychophysical conditions is not only in the interest of the employers, but still more of the employees; their working time can be reduced, their wages increased, their level of life raised. And above all, still more important than the naked commercial profit on both sides, is the cultural gain which will come to the total economic life of the nation, as soon as every one can be brought to the place where his best energies may be unfolded and his greatest personal satisfaction secured. The economic experimental psychology offers no more inspiring idea than this adjustment of work and psyche by which mental dissatisfaction in the work, mental depression and discouragement, may be replaced in our social community by overflowing joy and perfect inner harmony.

THE END

NOTES

NOTES

[1] (p. 10). The fullest account of the modern studies on individual differences is to be found in: William Stern: Die differentielle Psychologie in ihren methodischen Grundlagen. (Leipzig, 1911.)

[2] (p. 15). The practical applications of psychology in education, law, and medicine, I have discussed in detail in the books: Münsterberg: Psychology and the Teacher. (New York, 1910.) Münsterberg: On the Witness Stand. (New York, 1908.) (English edition under the title: Psychology and Crime.) Münsterberg: Psychotherapy. (New York, 1909.)

[3] (p. 41). Frank Parsons: Choosing a Vocation. (Boston, 1909.)

[4] (p. 42). M. Bloomfield: The Vocational Guidance of Youth. (Boston, 1911.)

[5] (p. 47). Vocations for Boys. (Issued by the Vocation Bureau of Boston. 1912.) Vocations for Boston Girls. (Issued by the Girls' Trade Education League. 1911.) Bulletins of Vocation Series. Issued by the Women's Educational and Industrial Union. 1911.)

[6] (p. 49). F. W. Taylor: The Principles of Scientific Management. (New York, 1911.) H. L. Gantt: Work, Wages, and Profits. (New York, 1912.) And the books of Emerson, Gilbreth, Goldmark, etc., to be mentioned later.

[7] (p. 52). H. Emerson: Efficiency as a Basis for Operation and Wages. (New York, 1912, p. 107.)

[8] (p. 52). H. Emerson: The Twelve Principles of Efficiency. (New York, 1912, p. 176.)

[9] (p. 53). H. Emerson: The Twelve Principles, p. 156.

[10] (p. 53). H. Emerson: The Twelve Principles, p. 177.

[11] (p. 54). F. W. Taylor: The Principles of Scientific Management, pp. 86–97.

[12] (p. 86). The experiments are being conducted and will be published by Mr. J. W. Bridges.

NOTES

[13] (p. 98). Investigation of Telephone Companies: Bureau of Labor. (Washington, Government Printing Office, 1910.)

[14] (p. 104). Ries: Beiträge zur Methodik der Intelligenzprüfung. (Zeitschrift für Psychologie, 1910, vol. 56.)

[15] (p. 112). For a survey of a large number of such tests and bibliography, compare: G. M. Whipple: Manual of Mental and Physical Tests. (Baltimore, 1911.)

[16] (p. 126). F. L. Wells: The Relation of Practice to Individual Differences. (American Journal of Psychology, 1912, vol. 23, pp. 75–88.)

[17] (p. 127). M. Bernays: Auslese und Anpassung der Arbeiterschaft der geschlossenen Grossindustrie, dargestellt an den Verhältnissen der Gladbacher Spinnerei und Weberei. (Leipzig, 1910, p. 337.)

[18] (p. 135). H. C. McComas: Some Types of Attention. (Psychological Review Monographs, vol. 13, 3, 1911.)

[19] (p. 149). Max Weber: Zur Psychophysik der industriellen Arbeit. (Archiv für Sozialwissenschaft und Sozialpolitik, 1908 and 1909, vols. 27 and 28.)

[20] (p. 150). Bryan and Harter: Studies in the Telegraphic Language. (Psychological Review, vol. 4.)

[21] (p. 151). W. F. Book: The Psychology of Skill. (University of Montana, Publications in Psychology, 1910.)

[22] (p. 156). H. Münsterberg: Beiträge zur experimentellen Psychologie. (Book IV, 1892.)

[23] (p. 156). A. J. Culler: Interference and Adaptability. (Archives of Psychology, 1912.)

[24] (p. 157). The experiments are being conducted and will be published by Mr. L. W. Kline.

[25] (p. 160). Adolf Gerson: Die physiologischen Grundlagen der Arbeitsteilung. (Zeitschrift für Sozialwissenschaft, 1907.)

[26] (p. 163). Karl Bücher: Arbeit und Rhythmus. (Fourth Edition, Leipzig, 1909, p. 438.)

[27] (p. 164). Frank G. Gilbreth: Motion Study. (New York, 1911.)

[28] (p. 166). Taylor: The Principles of Scientific Management. (New York, 1911, p. 71.)

NOTES

[29] (p. 169). The experiments are being conducted and will be published by Mr. E. R. Riesen.

[30] (p. 170). R. Herbertz: Zur Psychologie des Maschinenschreibens. (Zeitschrift für angewandte Psychologie, 1908, vol. 2, p. 551.)

[31] (p. 175). C. L. Vaughan: The Moter Power of Complexity. (Harvard Psychological Studies, vol. 2, 1906, p. 527.)

[32] (p. 177). G. M. Stratton: Some Experiments in the Perception of the Movement, Color, and Direction of Lights. (Psychological Review Monographs, vol. 10, 1908.)

[33] (p. 178). The experiments are being conducted and will be published by Miss L. M. Seeley.

[34] (p. 187). H. Münsterberg: Beiträge zur experimentellen Psychologie. (Book IV, 1892.)

[35] (p. 187). R. S. Woodworth: Accuracy of Voluntary Movement. (Psychological Review Monographs, vol. 3, 1899.)

[36] (p. 188). B. A. Lenfest: The Accuracy of Linear Movement. (Harvard Psychological Studies, vol. 2, 1906.)

[37] (p. 202). Ranschburg: Ueber die Bedeutung der Ähnlichkeit beim Erlernen, Behalten und bei der Reproduktion. (Journal für Psychologie und Neurologie, vol. 5.) Ranschburg: Zeitschrift für Psychologie und Physiologie der Sinnesorgane. (Vol. 30, 1902.)

[38] (p. 202). H. Kleinknecht: The Interference of Optical Stimuli. (Harvard Psychological Studies, vol. 2, 1906.)

[39] (p. 205). The experiments are being conducted and will be published by Miss O. E. Martin.

[40] (p. 210). Henry P. Kendall: Unsystematized, Systematized, and Scientific Management. (In Addresses and Discussions at the Conference on Scientific Management held at Dartmouth College, 1912.)

[41] (p. 213). Ernst Abbe: Gesammelte Abhandlungen. (Jena, 1908, vol. 3, p. 206.)

[42] (p. 214). A full survey of the problem and its literature is contained in: Josephine Goldmark: Fatigue and Efficiency. (New York, 1912.)

[43] (p. 217). F. W. Taylor: The Principles of Scientific Management. (New York, 1911, p. 58.)

315

NOTES

[44] (p. 223). W. Hellpach: Die geopsychischen Erschein-
ungen, Wetter, Klima und Landschaft und ihr Einfluss auf
das Seelenleben. (Leipzig, 1911, p. 176–212.)

[45] (p. 225). Aschaffenburg: Praktische Arbeit unter Alko-
holwirkung. (Psychologische Arbeiten — Kraepelin, vol. 1,
1906.)

[46] (p. 228). Hildebrand: Die Beeinflussung der Willens-
kraft durch den Alkohol. (Königsberg, 1910.)

[47] (p. 232). For the scientific facts concerning alcohol and
bibliography compare: Hugo Hoppe: Die Tatsachen über
den Alkohol. (Munich, 1912.)

[48] (p. 232). H. L. Hollingworth: The Influence of Caffein
on Mental and Motor Efficiency. (New York, 1912.)

[49] (p. 238). Levenstein: Die Arbeiterfrage. (Munich,
1912.)

[50] (p. 263). W. D. Scott: The Psychology of Advertising.
(Boston, 1908, p. 166.)

[51] (p. 269). D. Starch: Psychology of Preferred Positions.
(Judicious Advertising, New York, November, 1909.)

[52] (p. 275). C. T. Burnett: The Estimation of Number.
(Harvard Psychological Studies, vol. 2, p. 349.)

[53] (p. 285). E. S. Rogers: The Unwary Purchaser: A Study
in the Psychology of Trade Mark Infringement. (Michigan
Law Review, vol. 8, 1910.)

[54] (p. 292). The experiments are being conducted and will
be published by Mr. G. A. Feingold.

[55] (p. 299). W. D. Scott: Influencing Men in Business.
(New York, 1911.)

INDEX

INDEX

319

INDEX

INDEX

The Riverside Press
CAMBRIDGE . MASSACHUSETTS
U . S . A

CLASSICS IN PSYCHOLOGY

AN ARNO PRESS COLLECTION

Angell, James Rowland. **Psychology: On Introductory Study of the Structure and Function of Human Consciousness.** 4th edition. 1908

Bain, Alexander. **Mental Science.** 1868

Baldwin, James Mark. **Social and Ethical Interpretations in Mental Development.** 2nd edition. 1899

Bechterev, Vladimir Michailovitch. **General Principles of Human Reflexology.** [1932]

Binet, Alfred and Th[éodore] Simon. **The Development of Intelligence in Children.** 1916

Bogardus, Emory S. **Fundamentals of Social Psychology.** 1924

Buytendijk, F. J. J. **The Mind of the Dog.** 1936

Ebbinghaus, Hermann. **Psychology: An Elementary Text-Book.** 1908

Goddard, Henry Herbert. **The Kallikak Family.** 1931

Hobhouse, L[eonard] T. **Mind in Evolution.** 1915

Holt, Edwin B. **The Concept of Consciousness.** 1914

Külpe, Oswald. **Outlines of Psychology.** 1895

Ladd-Franklin, Christine. **Colour and Colour Theories.** 1929

Lectures Delivered at the 20th Anniversary Celebration of Clark University. (Reprinted from *The American Journal of Psychology,* Vol. 21, Nos. 2 and 3). 1910

Lipps, Theodor. **Psychological Studies.** 2nd edition. 1926

Loeb, Jacques. **Comparative Physiology of the Brain and Comparative Psychology.** 1900

Lotze, Hermann. **Outlines of Psychology.** [1885]

McDougall, William. **The Group Mind.** 2nd edition. 1920

Meier, Norman C., editor. **Studies in the Psychology of Art: Volume III.** 1939

Morgan, C. Lloyd. **Habit and Instinct.** 1896

Münsterberg, Hugo. **Psychology and Industrial Efficiency.** 1913

Murchison, Carl, editor. **Psychologies of 1930.** 1930

Piéron, Henri. **Thought and the Brain.** 1927

Pillsbury, W[alter] B[owers]. **Attention.** 1908

[Poffenberger, A. T., editor]. **James McKeen Cattell:** Man of Science. 1947

Preyer, W[illiam] **The Mind of the Child:** Parts I and II. 1890/1889

The Psychology of Skill: Three Studies. 1973

Reymert, Martin L., editor. **Feelings and Emotions:** The Wittenberg Symposium. 1928

Ribot, Th[éodule Armand]. **Essay on the Creative Imagination.** 1906

Roback, A[braham] A[aron]. **The Psychology of Character.** 1927

I. M. Sechenov: Biographical Sketch and Essays. (Reprinted from *Selected Works* by I. Sechenov). 1935

Sherrington, Charles. **The Integrative Action of the Nervous System.** 2nd edition. 1947

Spearman, C[harles]. **The Nature of 'Intelligence' and the Principles of Cognition.** 1923

Thorndike, Edward L. **Education:** A First Book. 1912

Thorndike, Edward L., E. O. Bregman, M. V. Cobb, et al. **The Measurement of Intelligence.** [1927]

Titchener, Edward Bradford. **Lectures on the Elementary Psychology of Feeling and Attention.** 1908

Titchener, Edward Bradford. **Lectures on the Experimental Psychology of the Thought-Processes.** 1909

Washburn, Margaret Floy. **Movement and Mental Imagery.** 1916

Whipple, Guy Montrose. **Manual of Mental and Physical Tests:** Parts I and II. 2nd edition. 1914/1915

Woodworth, Robert Sessions. **Dynamic Psychology.** 1918

Wundt, Wilhelm. **An Introduction to Psychology.** 1912

Yerkes, Robert M. **The Dancing Mouse** and **The Mind of a Gorilla.** 1907/1926